Life Lessons

Life Lessons

Things I Wish I'd Learned Earlier

LESLEY GARNER

HAY HOUSE

Australia • Canada • Hong Kong • India
South Africa • United Kingdom • United States

First published and distributed in the United Kingdom by:
Hay House UK Ltd, 292B Kensal Rd, London W10 5BE.
Tel.: (44) 20 8962 1230; Fax: (44) 20 8962 1239. www.hayhouse.co.uk

Published and distributed in the United States of America by:
Hay House, Inc., PO Box 5100, Carlsbad, CA 92018-5100. Tel.: (1) 760 431 7695 or (800)
654 5126; Fax: (1) 760 431 6948 or (800) 650 5115. www.hayhouse.com

Published and distributed in Australia by:
Hay House Australia Ltd, 18/36 Ralph St, Alexandria NSW 2015.
Tel.: (61) 2 9669 4299; Fax: (61) 2 9669 4144. www.hayhouse.com.au

Published and distributed in the Republic of South Africa by:
Hay House SA (Pty), Ltd, PO Box 990, Witkoppen 2068.
Tel./Fax: (27) 11 467 8904. www.hayhouse.co.za

Published and distributed in India by:
Hay House Publishers India, Muskaan Complex, Plot No.3, B-2,
Vasant Kunj, New Delhi – 110 070. Tel.: (91) 11 4176 1620;
Fax: (91) 11 4176 1630. www.hayhouse.co.in

Distributed in Canada by:
Raincoast, 9050 Shaughnessy St, Vancouver, BC V6P 6E5.
Tel.: (1) 604 323 7100; Fax: (1) 604 323 2600

A catalogue record for this book is available from the British Library.

ISBN 978-1-84850-066-2

Printed and bound in the UK by
TJ International, Padstow, Cornwall.

Acknowledgements

I am grateful to a lot of people for their contribution to this book. In particular I want to thank profoundly those many readers of the *Daily Telegraph* who have opened their hearts to me and entrusted me with their troubles and secrets. It is an honour and a privilege and I am truly sorry that I can give a considered answer to only some of them. But it is part of the ethos of my 'Lifeclass' column that the readers and I arrive at some kind of collective wisdom which we can all share, and I know, because people write and tell me so, that readers get a great deal out of reading other people's problems and the answers I give.

For giving me wise and essential support in advising others I want to thank Stuart Affleck. For putting me in this privileged position I thank Liz Hunt, who offered me the column in the first place. And I am also very grateful to my other regular editor, Susie Forbes of *Easy Living* and her former features editor, Lisa Markwell, who opened their pages to my column.

In particular I want to thank Susie for permission to reprint some of my *Easy Living* columns in this book.

This is a good place to say a public thank you to Guy, Anthony and Simon and the team at Pedalo who set up my very clear and elegant website,www.lesleygarner.com. I think it works beautifully and any fault in the running of it is all mine.

And finally I want to thank Michelle Pilley and the team at Hay House for their continued enthusiasm and support, which are exceptional. I realize, when I hear other writers grumbling about their publishers, how lucky I am with mine.

Contents

Introduction

This book draws on a lot of life experience. There is my own experience, which I distilled and filtered into three books, and then there is the experience of the thousands of readers who wrote to me when I became an advice columnist on a national newspaper, the *Daily Telegraph*.

I was offered the job as advice columnist partly because I had already written three books. The first one, *Everything I've Ever Done that Worked*, grew out of 20 years' experience of self-exploration and journalistic research. The idea came to me during a dark night of the soul when, stumbling about in my insomnia, I tripped over a pile of my own notebooks and began to read. What I realized was that the notebooks were full of useful stuff. Wouldn't it be a good idea, I thought as I sat on my bedroom floor at 4 in the morning, to go through all these notes, take out the useful stuff and put them between two covers? I meant to make this book for myself, as a companion and *aide-memoire* in sleepless moments, but a publishing friend thought this was a good idea too. It became a book of personal reflections, essays that I wanted to stimulate people's thinking, encourage and comfort them and also give them something practical to do when they felt stuck or lost. Nothing pleases me more than when I hear from readers who treat this book as it was intended to be, as friend and companion.

I so enjoyed writing this first book that I decided I would write two more. Love and relationships are fundamental to the experience of being human, so I wrote *Everything I've Ever Learned about Love*. In rebellion against the fixation with romantic and sexual love – but reflecting on that, too – I trawled my own life for love in every form – family, place, passions, friendship, children, art and nature and sex, of course. The book was revelatory and enriching for me to write and, I hope and am told, for people who read it.

When I looked about for the next great source of people's challenges, excitements and anxieties, I fell upon change. Life is change. There is no stillness, apart from the great stillness under everything which sustains everyone who seeks it out. *Everything I've Ever Learned about Change* set out to make a map of life's territory which would take the fear out of change, and also give techniques and tactics that would help people to make the changes they wanted in their own lives.

This book is an anthology of some of the essential pieces from all three of these books, but I am holding them up in a new light and giving them more depth and relevance by relating them to the extraordinary experience of being let into the confidence of thousands of people.

When I wrote my very first column for the *Daily Telegraph*, neither my editor nor I knew what to expect. We wanted to offer *Daily Telegraph* readers a place to bring their dilemmas, but we had none to kick off with. What shall I write? I asked my editor, Liz Hunt. Write about who you are and what you've done and why you're doing this, she said. So my first column was a kind of very public job application. It felt like diving off a high board into a very small swimming pool, without even knowing if there was any water in it. What would I do if nobody wrote in? But they did write in, with problems I had never even thought of.

I was overwhelmed, in those first months, with the responsibility of offering some kind of positive answer to the stories of marital breakdown, broken hearts, warring families, isolation, overload, mental despair, sickness and grief. I told myself that it was very good for a writer who had some pretensions to helping other people, to be forced to put her money where her mouth was. My books, while built on a belief that most human experiences are universal, drew on my *own* experience. Now I had to show people who were genuinely suffering that what I had learned had some relevance and hope for them.

There are different kinds of advice columnists. I admire terrifically the roll-up-your-sleeves, this-is-what-you-must-do-and-promise-me-you'll-do-it-right-now style of agony aunt who deals in certainties and solutions. I'm not like that in person and I'm not like that in the way I write. Doing this job made it clear to me, though, that I do have an approach and I do have strong underlying beliefs.

My approach is to treat a letter or an email as though I were reading tea leaves. There is the story somebody is telling you and the story they are *not* telling you, and I grew more skilled at reading between the words on the page. I enjoyed the sense of detective work. I became aware that each story had a number of characters and I was hearing only one voice. Often people will write in because they are anxious about another person – the child who is behaving badly, the parent who has remarried, the partner who wants to leave them. I resisted temptation to comment on the other person's behaviour and gently tried to make the writer see what part *they* were playing in their own drama because, however much we may feel we are a victim, the only person we can really change is ourselves.

I realized this was one of my core beliefs. We cannot manipulate others into behaving the way we want them to, but we can examine our own expectations and our own behaviour and make changes in those.

Another of my core beliefs is that we all know more than we think we do.

And the third core belief, which goes with this one, is that we need quiet, withdrawal and sometimes guidance to learn exactly what it is that we know.

We need to retreat into a corner of that great stillness, even for five minutes, for the waves of anger, resentment, fear, anxiety, grasping, desire, hurt and enraged blame of others to begin to subside and for the semblance of an answer to begin to emerge from our own depths. This shadow of a semblance of an answer might be no more than the immediate solution of stopping crying and going to bed. This is what happened to the writer Elizabeth Gilbert when she asked God for help in the middle of a nervous breakdown. In her book *Eat, Pray, Love*, she tells us that God did speak and what God said was simply, 'Go to bed, Elizabeth.' The answers we get can be very practical and down to earth.

Where can you find these moments of retreat, of stillness, of calm reflection, wise contemplation, spiritual, mental and emotional renewal?

Well, you can look in the obvious places: churches, temples, forests, mountaintops and deserts, meditation rooms and workshops. You can lock yourself in the bathroom and soak your troubles away. You can hose them down in the shower. You can go for a long run or bike ride, sit on a bus and stare out of the window or surrender to the elements on a beach. Or, no matter where you are, be it on the bus, the commuter train, a busy café or your own bed, you can do what millions of people do and find retreat, sustenance and renewal between the covers of a book.

And that is why I've written this one. When people wrote to me I often wanted to say to them, I can't mend your marriage or ease the pain of losing your child but I wrote something in a book once that I think you would find helpful or encouraging or that just might get you through the next five minutes.

And once you've got through the next five minutes you might feel a tiny shift that would get you through to lunchtime.

So I've made it easy. I have combined some of the most practical and inspiring pieces from my earlier books with answers I have written to readers which, I think, have a wider resonance. Reading one essay takes 30 seconds, but that one essay might shift you to a new way of being.

This book is designed to deliver what I know of mood-shifting, re-inspiring, creative thinking, re-framing your experience, shifting the dark and letting in light. You can apply it to work, love, grief, change, fear, even despair.

When you read it, know that it rests on four beliefs:

We cannot change others, only ourselves.

We know more than we think we do.

We find the answers in stillness.

And, the fourth truth, which I have learned from thousands of people – we are not alone. However awful you think your situation is, somebody has been there before you. Finding those others is a practical step, but finding the right book is a start. I hope this is the right book for you.

How to Use This Book

Everything in this book is meant to be useful, informative and inspiring, and to help you, the reader, become more aware of your own nature and the choices you make in life. Only the reader knows what he or she is looking for at any particular time, and there is a lot to be said for dipping into it at random. Each short chapter is meant to be read on its own and to offer some kind of insight or strategy to help understand and deal with what life throws at us.

Another way to read this book is to approach it when you want help with a particular problem. Your relationship might have broken up. You could be considering a major move or job change. You might find yourself overloaded and burnt out and simply wanting to get the zing back into life.

This is why I've designed a short-cut guide through the book, making suggestions and directing you straight to the chapter that might be most help to you. At the end of each chapter you will find suggestions of others which might relate to it and which could give you further help. For example, if you are at the painful end of a relationship you are likely to head straight for Seven-step Broken Heart Recovery Programme. At the end of this chapter you will find that I also suggest you read some more: Set Your Compass to Love, How Do You Know When It's Over?, Fatal Loyalty, The Beauty Way, and Singles and Their Habitat. One or two of these are directly to the point; others offer a fresh way of perceiving that might help dig you out of your despair.

Underlying all the letters and emails that are sent to me for my advice are bigger questions that will recur throughout any life, which is why I have loosely gathered the chapters together under five umbrella headings. These are: 'Who Am I?' – something people lose sight of on a regular basis; 'What Should I Be Doing?' – another question that crops up at regular intervals; 'Who Should I Be Doing It With?' – a question that covers anything which involves other people, from the love of one's life to caring for elderly parents. Then – because this happens at regular intervals, too, and gives rise to the most anguish – 'Where Did I Go Wrong?' followed by the pick-yourself-up-and-dust-yourself-down question, 'Now What Shall I Do?'

I am drawing on four sources: my advice column 'Lifeclass' as well as three previous books, *Everything I've Ever Done that Worked*, which offers life strategies, *Everything I've Ever Learned about Love*, which is about relationships, and *Everything I've Ever Learned about Change*, because life is always changing. So certain themes crop up. An underlying theme in all three books is caring for yourself in the midst of chaos. When you do this right, you can do more than ride the waves that keep coming – you can surf and soar.

What I really hope is that you enjoy the book and that you can return to it again and again and find fresh material which will help you live a richer and more conscious life.

Circuit breakers

There are six techniques in this book that I call 'Circuit Breakers'.

If you are in a panic, stuck in obsessive thinking, frozen by a difficult decision, don't see a way forward in the dark night of the soul, then, in my experience, these techniques will get you on to higher ground.

When I was cross-referencing this book I realized that one subject cropped up again and again and that was 'Gratitude' (page 9). Gratitude is really the most fundamental of practices. The worse you feel, the more important it is, because when things go wrong it is very easy to focus on gloom, but there is always something to be grateful for. Always. The less natural this feels, the more important it is to stop and give thanks for the smallest thing. You could be saving your own life.

Meditation is a simple, lifelong transformative practice that, once you have got the habit, will become as essential to you as cleaning your teeth. 'How to Meditate and Why' (page 35) will help to get you started.

'Writing a Letter to God' (page 41) can give you surprising and helpful insights.

'The Magic of 20 Minutes' (page 57) gets things done and moves you forward.

'The Beauty Way' (page 149) instantly touches your life with magic by revealing to you the beauty that lies everywhere.

And the partner to Gratitude is 'Forgiveness' (page 175). It's very hard, but this too will save your life. People who can't forgive are angry, bitter and old before their time, and their resentment poisons every aspect of their lives.

Let go. You are hurting only yourself.

Who Am I?

A psychotherapist friend says this is the question which underlies all the sessions he has with clients. I see it underlying anguished letters from people in all kinds of situations where they have lost an essential sense of self. I hear it from husbands and wives choking in abusive or loveless marriages. I hear it from people stuck in jobs which are stifling them. I hear it from people who have ended relationships which identified them and defined their future. I hear it from people struggling under the overwhelming responsibility of caring for others.

A sense of self and of kindness towards that self is essential to solving any problem. We are all kinder and nicer than we think, and quite desperate in our desire to be of help to others – but we are no help if we lose sight of ourselves. The first thing, as one reader wrote to me, is to *accept that you matter*. I hope that the following pieces give you some support for the essential business of shaping your own life.

Making a Life with Meaning

'Dear Lesley,' she wrote. 'From reading your answers I can see you are a wise person. That's why I am writing to you. I am 49 years old. I married at 19, have a large family, all grown up, some married, the others studying abroad. My husband is busy with his job and also doing acts of kindness for people.

'Me, I'm literally doing nothing the whole day. I am lonely. I am also isolated. I don't have any contact with other people whatsoever. The days go by with me looking at the Internet or taking a walk. I hardly talk to my husband and I feel there is an ocean between us. When he comes home and tells me bits and pieces of his day, I nod but I haven't got anything to say.

'He is a very good man but he is a man and not really interested in what I read or in what my opinions are.

'Gosh, it's getting worse. I know that the mind should be busy but with what? Please don't tell me to get a hobby. I try hobbies. At the moment I am learning bookbinding and I've done years of calligraphy. Please don't tell me to do volunteer work. I go out with an old lady once a week for one hour.

'I just can't volunteer in the old people's home because it depresses me.

'Then you'll probably tell me to go and take a course. OK. I've done that.

'And then what? You see, you can't just do hobbies, volunteer work and courses from morning to night.

'You might tell me to get a job but I'm not going to start knocking on doors at my age to look for work. The rejection, the "Sorry, no job available" would simply erode the last of my self-confidence. Please tell me what I should do because I'm really desperate. Eloise.'

I nearly didn't answer Eloise's letter because, to be perfectly honest, it exasperated me. We've all had friends going through a bad patch who beg for help and advice and then stonewall you with a barrage of defensive rejections of everything you suggest. They – like Eloise – crouch behind a wall of negativity, calling out for help but ducking down behind the wall as soon as you suggest a way around it.

But, somehow, her letter stuck in my mind. For a start, I could tell that she was really unhappy. Second, she painted me a clear picture of a certain kind of mid-life crisis – and a typically female mid-life crisis at that. She simply didn't know who she was any more. She married straight out of school before she had to make an independent way in the world. She became a mother, over and over it seems, and the next 30 years went by in a blur of home-running and child-rearing. Then, at 49, her children had gone and her husband functioned perfectly well in the world while she –

well, who is she? Thirty years ago she ducked this question by submerging herself in others, but now the question is urgent.

I was actually excited for Eloise. If she wanted to take up the challenge, she was on the brink of a great quest, the ultimate human adventure, the search for meaning. If this applies to you too – and I think it applies to all of us – I am going to suggest to you, as I suggested to her, that this quest has seven stages and I will tell you what they are.

Before you can get a life you must support, protect and sustain it, so stages one, two and three on the road to meaning are practical and physical.

You need shelter, security and sustenance. Without a roof, a lock on your door and food on your table, any higher purpose is difficult to achieve and all your efforts will go into the grind of simply staying alive. Eloise had a home and food on her table, thanks to the good man who was her husband, and she still felt lost. There is a higher phase in the search for meaning when, like a Buddhist monk with a begging bowl, we could choose to turn our back on security and set out on a spiritual search. Very few of us tread this path and yet, like Eloise, we sense that simple physical existence isn't enough.

She wanted more. She was materially satisfied but unhappy. She needed to look at the next four aspects to building a life with meaning: the physical, the emotional, the intellectual and the spiritual. To live fully you must satisfy the body, the heart, the mind and the spirit.

The depression that comes with loss of meaning can be alleviated by activating the body. It was made to be used, to move, to dance, to run, to swim, to climb. Get out of breath. Use your senses. The sense of touch unites us with others. Have a massage. Stroke a cat. The senses of taste, smell, sight, hearing connect us to the world. Next time you go for a walk, activate your senses. Notice what you hear and see, smell the world like an animal. Touch the grass, a tree, a stone. Bring yourself alive.

But that isn't enough. Human beings need the love, affection and connection of others. Joining with others, in a family, a sports team, in a choir, round a dinner table, gives life meaning. Eloise's heart, with the absence of her children and her sense of separation from her husband, was lonely but it needn't have been. There are many ways to activate your heart.

The woman in the house nearest to yours is probably as lonely as you. Invite her round. Touch your husband with affection if you feel you have nothing to say. Find out more about the people you come into contact with. They are suffering too. A full family life can lead to a neglect of friendship. When family life changes, friends are even more important.

How many people, like Eloise, suffer from boredom? That is because their intellect is not fed. Life will have no meaning for you if you are not interested. If you reject the idea of courses, that is because you have not found a course which stimulates and excites you. When people complain to me of a lack of interest in life, that makes me suspect depression because life is endlessly interesting and exciting. Read. Walk. Observe.

Above all, *learn*. When you were a child I bet you were excited and curious. What was it you were excited and curious about when you were ten years old? Revisit it. Also, seek company. Your mind will be much more alive if you pursue your interests with other people, maybe with old friends, maybe with the new ones you will inevitably make as you wake up to meaning.

But no search for meaning is complete without the seventh stage, the stage of the spirit. You don't have to believe in God, though you may have a religious belief and that may be what gives meaning to your life. It is enough to have a sense of what the 12-step programmes call a 'higher power', something bigger than ourselves. For me that means the mystery of nature and the universe, the power of the imagination, art, music, the scientific pursuit of truth. Bookbinding and calligraphy, which were Eloise's chosen crafts, can be spiritual as well as practical pursuits. So is any dedication to an art, a craft or a skill.

If anyone is in quest of meaning in their lives, I suggest you read an excellent book called *The Happiness Hypothesis* by Jonathan Haidt (Heinemann). And I suggest you get together with someone you trust and scan those moments in your lives when you felt truly alive, and try to understand what links them. This golden thread can lead you forward into a future that is as fulfilling as the best bits of your past.

See also Writing a Letter to God, The Power of Gratitude, The Art of Self-reinvention, Set Your Compass to Love

The Power of Gratitude

There are two regular practices which can transform your attitude to and experience of life. One is gratitude. The other is forgiveness. They are the housekeeping tools of the mind and heart. One can fill you with a sense of the richness of life. The other cleans the dark and destructive corners of resentment, anger and hurt that accumulate, sometimes on a daily basis. If you are really down it can be difficult to practise either, but it is probably easier to switch your focus to gratitude than it is to forgive people who are hurting you.

Gratitude is always a good place to start from in the middle of turmoil. It is like a light which you can carry at will from the good places in your life to the dark places. It will illuminate them.

Gratitude begins as an instinctive, unfettered and free-flowing response to the good moments in life. When we are children it begins as a sense of awe and love, before we are taught to say 'Thank you.' Then we sometimes find ourselves being made to say 'Thank you,' politely, for things we are not at all grateful for, so the sensation and the state get muddled. But you can find gratitude again. Remember the experience of receiving a spoonful of delicious ice-cream, a sip of complex wine, an eyeful of moonlight, the sight of the sea, a tender touch, a helping hand or the clean embrace of your own bed, whether it contains a teddy bear, a lover or simply rest at the end of a long and tiring day. Gratitude, unforced, will overwhelm you.

Remember those moments when you are in a beautiful place, in beautiful light, in beautiful weather, and all the goodness of the world seems to be spread unstintingly before you. You know, in every cell of your body, that it is sensational to be alive. Your whole self expands to receive your good fortune.

Remember those moments when you can hardly believe your luck. You have met someone wonderful who, miraculously, seems to think you are wonderful too. Or you find yourself in the heart of a group of friends, sustained by cheerfulness and good humour, and you think how lucky you are to have them. You lose a child in the supermarket and, after a heart-stopping minute, you find them again. That is gratitude.

Remember those moments when you are part of a crowd enjoying an extraordinary experience. Your team is scoring a winning goal. You are watching a great performance of an exciting play. At a concert you are all on your feet, moving in time with the music. You will never forget it. You are so lucky to be here.

Narrow your focus. Remember the time you had a cold and somebody made you a hot drink. Remember the time you were stranded and somebody offered you a timely lift. Remember when the money to pay a debt came just in time. Remember the stranger who helped you carry a heavy bag up the stairs. These are simple, everyday things, but they connect you with the flow of the world.

Everyone knows what gratitude is, what the sensation feels like. The trick in the conscious practice of gratitude is to reach into this emotional store and be grateful on purpose.

In moments of stress and depression it is far easier to follow a damaging practice of ingratitude, resentment, rage and blame. But these obsessive, negative thoughts switch on the chemicals in our bodies which damage our immune system and lead to states of depression and despair. The focus switches from the simple things we have to the innumerable things we don't have, even though others do. Ironically, the more we have, the more we want. But wise people, from the Buddha to the sociologists who have identified the modern sickness of 'luxury envy', know that want and desire can never be satisfied. The things we think we want are actually the sources of our unhappiness.

The trick is to identify this pattern of thought, and change it as soon as it occurs. Reach into your store at moments of trial and despair and apply the transformative balm of gratitude to your open wounds.

It seems impossible. You have real problems. Of course you have, but they won't be any easier to solve if you focus only on the damage they are doing to you. Negativity, self-pity, complaints are addictive, easy and irresistible. They darken vision so that hope and goodness are invisible. They are also a habit.

I have found that if I practise the habit of gratitude instead, starting with the smallest thing (and nothing is too small), my attitude can be swiftly transformed. I like the practice of Mother Teresa, who treated everything that came to her as a gift. 'Excuse me, Mother Teresa,' said one of her nuns when they faced a long weary delay at an airport. 'We have the gift of several hours' wait.' Advanced practitioners of gratitude can look on everything that happens to them – sickness, accident, bereavement, poverty – as a gift. They are the people who look back at a disaster and say, 'Oddly enough, that was one of the best things that ever happened to me.'

If you really want to feel enormous gratitude for your messy, problematic life, try nearly losing it. I have never felt so abundantly, humbly, unstintingly grateful, so in love with my life, as I did immediately after surviving a car crash. If your problems aren't life-threatening you can change your attitude to them by practising gratitude for the smallest things. And the moment to do this is when you find yourself feeling least grateful. Stop right there and say the simple words *thank you.*

See also The Beauty Way, The Freedom of Forgiveness, When the Sea Is Rough, Mend Your Sails

Living Your Own Life

Paul wrote to me because he was trapped in his position in a family business. His father was overbearing, his older brother was a bully and, even though Paul and his brothers had been running the business together for over 15 years, he felt victimized and out of control of his own life.

He longed to change but was incapable of expressing any negative feelings.

'You may be surprised to learn,' he wrote, 'that I am a calm type of person, not prone to losing my temper, but maybe I should.'

I wasn't at all surprised that Paul thought he was a very calm person. It is often the outwardly calm people who are sitting on a boiling volcano of unexpressed anger and resentment. It is much better to learn how to express anger than to succumb to a nervous breakdown or a heart attack further down the line. Many, many people struggle along trying to lead a life which is not really their own, only to have the changes they are resisting made for them by illness, redundancy or death. If you learn how to take control of your own life, you could also be saving it.

I was frustrated with Paul. Who was going to inhabit his own life if he wouldn't? People who are blaming their problems on the rest of their family need to understand that none of the characters in a family drama has their interests at heart. None of them can see inside your head. Paul saw himself in the role of victim, but it didn't really matter whether this was the part he had been given or one he had chosen and created for himself. The point of being a victim is that it is a role that has to be accepted and, once accepted, is one in which the victim can become word- and thought-perfect. It's a role that can become so refined and consolidated that nobody – not the family, not the victim him- or herself – can see that person in any other part.

The difficulty of rewriting a script as ingrained as this is that, for Paul, it was not just about changing his job but about challenging his family, constructing a new identity and upending his whole life. Personal revolution is a high-risk business. You could lose everything – or you could find that, once the dust had settled, your life and your relationships have improved. The choice is between the great fear of making a major change or dwindling slowly towards old age in a perpetual simmer of resentment and unfulfilment. If you shy away from change, you risk not only being unhappy in yourself but a cause of unhappiness to others. I could never recommend that.

So how do you begin to make the deep-rooted changes that are needed when you want to take back control of your own life? I didn't recommend therapy to Paul because I could see years pass while he spent money explaining to a therapist why his life was so grim. I did recommend assertiveness training, because this teaches you practical skills in expressing yourself clearly without resorting to outright aggression or to the kind of passive-aggressive silent treatment that I suspect Paul used. Assertiveness training helps in dealings with family and work colleagues and would give Paul the skills he could carry over into a new job.

I also recommended a course called the Hoffman Process, just in case Paul felt he really wanted to go for broke in confronting his entire relationship with his family in a way that would put him back in touch with the person he'd really like to be, as well as increasing his understanding of and compassion for them. Often the people we see as victimizing us are victims themselves. I have done the Hoffman Process myself and you can learn more about it on their website,www.hoffmaninstitute. co.uk. In their own words, it is an 'eight-day intensive residential course in which you are skilfully and compassionately shown how to let go of the past, release pent-up stress, self-limiting behaviours and resentments and start creating the future you desire'.

I wasn't sure that Paul was ready to leap so far out of his comfort zone, so I also recommended a small change. He comforted himself by listening to classical music, which is good, but I recommended that he widened his repertoire by listening to unfamiliar music, music which expresses the difficult emotions of life, music that gets the blood racing and expands the brain. Chumbawumba's anthem 'I get knocked down but I get up again,' I suggested, was the perfect mood music for turning worms.

See also Stepping Stones, Knowing What You Want and Asking for It, Fatal Loyalty, The Power of Gratitude, The Freedom of Forgiveness

How to Change Your Self-image

There's one very English expression that always makes me laugh when I hear it. It's when people say, 'Oh, no, thank you. I'm not really a biscuit person.' Or, 'I'll have tea, thank you. I'm not really a coffee person.' Our world is full of tea people, coffee people, cheese-and-biscuit people or, if we really want to widen our horizons, beach people or book people. It's curious how we identify ourselves with things as banal as coffee and biscuits, yet there's a self-satisfaction in the way people trot out this phrase, as though they are very happy to identify themselves by a simple little habit.

We are very undemanding in the way we like to see ourselves, but I'd like to suggest that life could become much more exciting if we got a lot braver. A new image could be so much more than a new haircut.

There is something very exhilarating, as well as scary, in stepping right outside the comfort zone. The words you want to aim for are, 'If my friends could see me now.' If they could see me hang-gliding off this cliff edge, sailing above them in this balloon. If they could see me running this marathon or about to dive off the side of this boat. If my friends could see me attempting to dance salsa in Cuba when I've never been a dancing person. If they could see me trying out my newly learned Turkish on this fisherman when I've always been a two-weeks-in-the-Dordogne person.

Be very aware of what you say when you describe yourself. What limitations are you putting on yourself? How are you holding yourself down?

Is your image of yourself fixed in some outgrown life, maybe even a life that somebody else has designed for you? I get many letters from people who are festering in a life which once offered a line of least resistance, a life which pleased their parents and followed the line laid down by some outgrown partner. They long to be somebody different but they are not a running-away sort of person and wonder desperately what to do.

The letters I get from the people who have run away tend to be much happier. These people have burned their boats and are warming their hands in the glow. This is just as well, as they are usually poorer and maybe have trouble with the heating bills, but their self-image has changed dramatically. They have made the biggest change of all: from victim to protagonist.

Self-image is not about the clothes you wear. It is about the actions you take – or shy away from. Being proactive, in whatever area of your life, is the most certain way I know to experience yourself as an entirely different – a more interesting, a more exciting, a more impressive – person.

People always think that a change has to be dramatic and radical, and sometimes that can work, but for those of you out there still identifying yourself by the biscuits you eat or the tea you drink, a change of self-image can be as attainable as a simple change of brand. A green-tea person is different from an Earl Grey person and, who knows, drinking green tea might lead to an experiment with sushi. A sushi person might go exploring in a different part of town and, who knows, go into different shops, an art gallery, a cultural event. Once your horizons start expanding there is no stopping them, and being adventurous in a cultural and culinary way is just as exciting, I think, as being adventurous in a physical and challenging way. Adventures, of whatever kind, can lead to a dramatic change of self-image.

And a change of self-image leads, inexorably, to a difference in the way the world treats you. Things that don't change and stay small are invisible.

Surprise people and they begin to look at you in a new way. Cinderella in a party frock gets invited to the ball. She gets seen by a handsome prince.

You, with your new interest in contemporary art or Old Church Slavonic or ice hockey, will find doors opening for you. One thing leads to another – new opportunities, new journeys, new friends. There's one guaranteed thing about horizons. As soon as you reach one, another one opens up before you.

The journey begins with you catching yourself out in the act of boxing yourself in. Would you like to try this red wine? Don't say, 'I'm not a red wine person.' Say, 'Thank you – where does it come from? Have you been there?' A door opens. From a person who says 'no' you have become a person who says 'yes', and that makes all the difference.

See also Is It Ever Too Late to Change?, Stepping Stones, The Art of Self-reinvention

Being Your Own Best Friend

I have this person who follows me about all day, hurling insults.

'Idiot!' she exclaims when I delete the wrong email. 'No will powers,' she sneers when, under no pressure at all, I order the extra glass of wine or agree to have the dessert I'd told myself I was going to turn down.

'Lazybones!' she shrieks, if I turn over for an extra five minutes in bed.

It's very wearing, this constant undermining barrage of put-downs and curses.

Oddly enough, even though she is so severe and critical, she doesn't succeed in making me modify my behaviour and she certainly doesn't build up my confidence or make me feel good about myself in any way. And yet I find it very hard to shake her off.

Compare her with my real best friends – and luckily I have quite a few. These wonderful men and women appreciate me when I've made an effort to look good, and even tell me I look great when this other person has looked in the mirror in scorn. They tell me I'm doing a great job when this other person has despaired of my ever getting it right. They listen to my woes without agreeing with me (or with this other person) that I have every reason to doubt myself. On the contrary, these lovely people tell me to relax, that I'm being too hard on myself. They remind me of things I have done that worked, of places I've been that make me happy. I associate them with good times and bright visions, while this other person only ever reminds me of failures and broken dreams.

The thing is, this other person is me. She is an agglomerate of all the negative judgements, midnight terrors and critical harshness that I have ever experienced, and then some. And the really mad thing is that she is the one I pay most attention to. When she has control over my brain I can take the kindest compliment, devalue, dismiss and crush it under foot. 'Oh, you're only saying that to cheer me up,' I think. And what, exactly, is wrong with that?

Most of us, unless we are lucky enough to be fantastically optimistic, carry this dark critic inside us. One of the arts of living well is to notice it and turn down the volume. In order to be happy and successful, we need to replace this corrosive onslaught with the kinder voices that offer us patience and encouragement.

Imagine that you are taking care of a small child. Unless you are some Dickensian villain, you do not attack this small child's confidence with withering criticism. If she spills something, you laugh and say it's only an accident. You try to minimize her distress. When he does a drawing you find something to love about it. You don't tell him that his drawing is rubbish, because you know that's the way to destroy his joy in painting. When she feels shy or unhappy, you cuddle and tease and coax her. Why can't we behave in this essentially kind way with our own selves?

The dark side of ourselves, this withering inner voice, can be challenged and replaced with something more merciful, more nurturing. If we pay attention to the way we talk to ourselves in private, we can learn to correct the harshness and become our own best friend. This isn't New Age twaddle, it's a way of changing the quality of your life. It doesn't mean that you cease being self-critical – we need to be self-critical in order to improve – but it does mean that we learn sometimes to give ourselves a pat on the back, and that we hold back on the insults.

Think of the kindest person you know, the most encouraging teacher, the most loving mother. That is the voice you want to encourage in your own head. When you make a mess of a task, don't shout at yourself and hurl insults. Less of the 'Idiot!' Would you address a friend like that? Sit back. Tell yourself, without heat, that you haven't got it right this time, but congratulate yourself for trying. Then suggest to yourself that you have another go, maybe trying something differently. Tell yourself that you know you can do it, and gently remind yourself of some past success.

And finally, if you really want to see your inner monster for what it is, take a piece of paper and write down, without pausing to think, all the rude, destructive and negative things you hurl at yourself in your own mind.

Would you give houseroom to this person in real life? Of course not. It's time to get them right out of your head for ever.

See also My Samurai Partner, The Power of the People, Facing Fear, The Freedom of Forgiveness

Getting Conscious at 30

Andy was 31 and he was like a surfer stranded on a beach. All those waves that carry you through your twenties – ambition, sexual drive, social opportunities – had swept him irresistibly into a relationship of convenience with an equally driven and ambitious girl. They were both so busy they hardly saw each other, but that seemed to suit both of them. He liked and admired her a lot, but neither of them wanted to move in with each other or have kids. Going with the flow was what got them involved with each other but, for Andy, the flow had slowed down. He was sitting bemused on the beach of his life, as thousands do in their thirties, looking around him and wondering how he'd got there.

Three years had passed and he was still with the same woman. 'Deep down,' he wrote, 'I'd like to break out and have something new in my life. I have never been in the dating scene in my life. All I have ever done was work hard. Even in my teens I played sports at a high level and I feel like I have missed out a lot and would love to just go out on dates and have all the fun

I've never had. Instead I have a career, property, very healthy finances. I wonder if I made a huge sacrifice in my twenties.

'I wonder whether I should just stop thinking too much and appreciate the great partner I have or whether I owe myself all those experiences which should be part of the growing-up process in every adult's life. Shall I listen to my heart or to my brain? Andy.'

I really responded to Andy's letter, because it encapsulated all that 30-year-old angst of 'How did I get here? Is this where I want to be? Where am I going? Help!' And I also felt really excited for him, because I saw this as the point at which he could really begin to live his life with awareness and intention, and not just because he had been carried forward on a wave of education, training, hard work and blind instinct.

Andy thought he was drowning, but I saw him as coming to life. His relationship either needed to end or it needed to take time out for really serious and honest discussion about what they both really wanted out of life. The chances were that the relationship wouldn't survive this kind of scrutiny, and then what? I didn't see the dating scene satisfying Andy for long. This is stuff people do in their teens and twenties, when their capacity for self-knowledge and reflection is minimal. In your thirties you are looking to make more sense of your life.

So I recommended a book called *Eat, Pray, Love* by an American writer called Elizabeth Gilbert. She found herself, at about Andy's age, with a broken marriage and in a spiritual and emotional crisis. She decided to devote a year to exploring different aspects of her life. She'd always wanted to learn Italian, so she set off to Italy, where she also ate huge amounts of delicious Italian food and put back all the weight she'd lost in her nervous breakdown. She then went to find God in an Indian ashram. And, finally, she set off to Bali to apprentice herself to a traditional healer but found, after a year where she combined celibacy and spiritual quest with a whole-hearted, sensual opening up to life, a real human love instead.

What I said to Andy is that, at his age, this isn't just an emotional crisis. I think it is a spiritual one as well. It's not just about dating and catching up on teenage fun. It's about giving your life meaning.

If this is you, have you thought of taking a sabbatical? More and more people take time out in mid-career to travel, volunteer, explore themselves and the huge world they are missing out on. It sounded as though Andy could afford to do something as radical as that. It sounded as though, with his sporting and career experience, he had a lot to give. I thought his girlfriend, who sounded like more of a friend, would understand that.

We all of us reach places in our lives where the tramlines we have been unconsciously following run out and we find we are not where we wanted to be. Sometimes it works to get on a whole different tram – or better, get out and walk. It's normal to be unconscious and instinctual through our teens and twenties, but as you enter your thirties it's time to begin looking for the bigger picture, one that doesn't involve a choice between head and heart but combines them – and makes room for the spirit, too. And as for obeying your head or your heart, you'll never know what they are saying if you don't make time to listen to them. And don't panic. This stuff takes a lifetime.

See also The Art of Self-reinvention, Writing a Letter to God, The Research and Development Fund, Love vs Space – the New Infidelity

A Short Guide to the Subconscious

I believe that many projects fail because some unacknowledged part of ourselves is not on board. Jostling about under the surface of a well-ordered mind is a crowd of unexamined ideas that, collectively, can sink the proud ship of your hopes like the iceberg holing the unsinkable *Titanic*. It follows that if you want to change your life, it helps to become acquainted with your subconscious.

You know your subconscious mind may be operating against you when you have strange dreams. You suspect its influence when you apply your conscious mind fully to a project and yet are ineffective. You can detect its presence when you make silly errors even when you thought you were in control. It is probably no accident that you post the uncensored letter and throw your careful rewrite into the bin.

You know your subconscious mind may be operating in your favour when you suddenly put two and two together and make five. You suspect unseen forces are operating when the perfect book jumps off the library shelf. You can be sure your subconscious mind is at work when you fall asleep with a problem and wake up with a solution.

Once you become aware of the ways in which your subconscious mind works, the next step is to harness its power on purpose. I believe that we should all become skilled at connecting with our unconscious mind because the best decisions are made by a mind cooperating with itself. Here's a short history and geography of your unconscious to help you find it.

In some ways the unconscious is a 20th-century invention. Before Sigmund Freud reached down into the dark recesses of his patients' minds, people had found other explanations for the forces of unreason in their lives. Mostly they thought of them as gods. If plans went awry, ships were wrecked and wars raged out of control, that was because Apollo or Athene or Aphrodite was miffed and wanted to make things hot for humans. You could attempt to appease the gods, but they were essentially capricious. They were there to relieve you of any illusions that you were the master of your fate. They specialized in punishing hubris, the overweening pride that affects people who think that they have everything under control, with a deflating shot of nemesis, the nasty comeuppance that punishes pride in the end.

The idea of fate as an external force over which man had no control held sway for the next couple of thousand years. Then along came Freud and examined the random ragbag of contradictory ideas and symbols that came up out of his patients' minds when they stopped censoring themselves. He asked himself, could it be that we are somehow creating trouble for ourselves? Could the forces of sabotage be right inside us?

We have taken Freud's view of things ever since, more or less, though his followers, especially Carl Jung, developed and changed his ideas. Freud thought of the subconscious as a kind of cellar where we threw all the bad and inadmissible urges, particularly the sexual ones, that 19th-century Viennese society rejected. Jung's cellar was much bigger than Freud's and it had underground tunnels linking it up with all the other human cellars in one great collective unconscious. We weren't just driven by hidden factors in our own lives. No, we were all affected by the collective taboos of our history and culture.

The huge power the unconscious has over us comes from repression. It is the subversive power of the hidden and unknown. The surface problem may be that you have difficulty getting a job, but your lack of success may stem from a lack of belief in your own worth, which in turn may come from messages you may have taken in and buried in your own cellar as a child. And these may originate from a collective belief in your family that to rise above your station is to invite jealousy, even retribution. If you sabotage yourself, then you will not break your family taboo. That is a heavy burden to carry into the interview room.

So how do you let the light into your own unconscious? Better, how do you harness its benevolent power? A long-term approach is to consider psychoanalysis, the therapeutic method developed by Freud, but it is expensive and takes a long time. Plenty of methods of psychotherapy exist, however, which create less dependency and cost less money but still provide the space and listening which will bring unconscious fears and wishes into the light.

There are also many workshops and processes that will give you access to your unconscious mind and the more complete self-knowledge which follows. In the Hoffman Process, for example, they use the psychological model of a fourfold self: an emotional self, an intellectual self, a spiritual self and the body. When you learn to address each one in turn you see how often your internal selves are at odds, particularly the emotional and the intellectual selves. The intellectual self is often the bully shouting, 'Go on!' or 'Don't you dare!' while the emotional self hangs back and says, 'Shan't!' or 'But I'd really like to.' No action comes out of these impasses.

If you are resistant to the idea of psychotherapy or workshops but would still like to change the areas of your life that are not working, it is worth sitting down calmly and asking yourself what you have to gain from things going wrong. There is always something to be gained from staying stuck in even the most difficult circumstances. Repeated patterns create a perverse comfort, the comfort of the familiar. If bad behaviour was what got you attention as a child, then you may think bad behaviour is worth repeating as a way of making people pay attention to you.

Even if the benefits of change are obvious to the rational mind, like weight loss or a better job, don't underestimate the irrational resistance to change. If you change you could attract retribution or envy, and this unacknowledged fear will make any escape attempt half-hearted. It is the power of the gods we are dealing with, after all.

The unconscious loves anything that isn't rational or prosaic. It won't give up its secrets if you harangue it, but it will respond to art and music and poetry. It likes to slip ideas into your mind when you are half-focused on something else. It loves to pop up on journeys or in idle moments, which is why some people rely on the three Bs – bed, bus and bath – as places where inspiration can strike. I would add 'beach', if you get the chance to walk on one. Beaches free the mind.

Contacting the unconscious mind can be huge fun. It is a rich and endlessly fascinating place, not just the dark cellar of Freud's speculations. There are many roads to it and the treasure we find there is our own. It can be what makes us whole.

See also Made in Error, How to Be Creative, Living Your Own Life, Fatal Loyalty

How to Meditate and Why

People who have no experience of meditation tend to think that it is a matter of sitting and letting your mind go blank. On the contrary. Meditation is the practice of unswerving concentration. It is an intense mental discipline and that is what makes it such a valuable tool in the decluttering of the mind and the destressing of the heart.

Meditation, for those who have embraced it, is as essential to their functioning as *barre* practice to a ballet dancer or scales to a musician. Without it there is no internalized self-discipline to hold everything else together. It was the Dalai Lama who said, 'The more I have to do, the more I meditate.' Meditation means replacing useless fretting and random worrying with a thought-free mental space which allows renewal and change.

The baby meditator has just as much trouble meditating as a baby pianist might have trying to play Beethoven. I am not as regular or as disciplined a meditator as I might be, so this is what often happens when I sit down to meditate. I close my eyes. I focus my attention on the sensation of my breathing.

I use a simple sequence of phrases I learned in a retreat led by the Zen Buddhist monk Thich Nhat Hanh. Breathing in, I know that I am breathing in. Breathing out, I know that I am breathing out. Breathing in, I remember that I didn't finish clearing up the kitchen, which leads me to the fact that we've run out of bread and before I know it my mind is racing down the high street and into the supermarket. I pull myself up. I focus again on my breath. Breathing in, I am breathing in. Breathing out, I am out tonight because I'm meeting friends for a drink. I must remember to return that book I borrowed and would I be better taking the car, which means finding somewhere to park, and my friend got towed away last time, which means a £200 fine, and ... I focus on my breath again.

And so it goes. And so goes everyone. Controlling thoughts is like herding cats. Push them out and they come right back through the cat flap, bringing other stray cats with them. That is why we need to meditate.

When my mind is at its most random and overloaded, victim of the need to multi-task, active in a frantic way like a randomly disfunctioning radio tuner, that is when I need to meditate. When I have a sensation of anxiety deep inside, a feeling that I daren't stop, that is when I need to meditate. When I realize that my thoughts, perhaps about another person or a relationship that is in trouble, are obsessive and repetitive, that is when I need to meditate.

To meditate is to return to a state of still potential out of which organization and order can grow. And it can help order us on the physical level, too. I know for a fact, because I check it, that meditation immediately lowers my blood pressure.

Like all regular practices, meditation can create long-term changes in attitude and behaviour. The regular experience of internal stillness and calm creates a recognition and knowledge of the state that can draw you back in times of turmoil. People who are meditators have a tool that can prevent them from acting out their inner turbulence in a way which harms themselves and others. This is why meditation can be so effective when it is taught in prisons and workplaces.

There are many, many ways to meditate. By this I mean ways to attain a state of inner focus and concentration. Musicians, dancers, sports people, crafts people, children lost in a game, anyone whose work requires concentration knows what it is like to get into a meditative state. But the meditative state can be experienced anywhere. The ultimate aim of mindfulness meditation is to make each moment of daily life – preparing breakfast, doing the dishes – an act of mindfulness. By 'mindfulness' I mean nothing more complex, or more difficult, than the simple art of doing and thinking about one thing at a time.

If you have never tried meditation, here is a very simple way to begin. It is the way I always follow. Find a quiet, undisturbed place to sit. Sit upright. Relax your hands loosely on your knees. Close your eyes. Become aware of your breathing. Simply concentrate on your breath without attempting to control it. Be aware of the sensation of the incoming breath in your nostrils, in your throat, in the rise of your ribs and stomach. When the impulse to release the breath occurs naturally, simply observe the same process in reverse. That is all. Simply observe, without interference, the sensations of your own breathing.

The breath is there to save you from distraction. Hardly will you have started this simple process than your mind will take you anywhere but where you are trying to be, within yourself at this particular moment. It is shocking how hard it is to focus on one simple thing. It is humiliating how easy it is for the unconscious chain reaction of our own random thoughts to take charge of the space of our mind.

But our thoughts are not in charge of our mind. We are. Meditation is the process of discovering, isolating and strengthening this 'we', this 'I', this calm, detached, compassionate observer that need not be swept away in the chaos of our lives. Meditation is the art of building an inner lighthouse to guide us home in the turbulence.

See also When the Sea Is Rough, Mend Your Sails, The Beauty Way, Writing a Letter to God, The Power of Gratitude, The Freedom of Forgiveness

What Should I Be Doing?

I don't know what you should be doing with your life, but I do know that it is a question that recurs on a daily basis, and I do know some strategies that will help you find clarity.

There is a lot of fear and panic around this question. It could be the adolescent panic of thinking you are a failure before you start. Or it could be the grown-up panic of feeling stuck and that you have left everything too late. I think it is a really exciting question, because we are freer than we think to shape our own lives and it can take decades to shake off the weight of our education and the expectations of others before we dare try that thing we've wanted to do all along. The following chapters may give you some help in dealing with the panic, in finding ways to tap into your own innate desires, and some practical strategies for achieving them.

Writing a Letter to God

I got this idea from Spiritual Fitness coach Caroline Reynolds, who uses it in her workshops. If you don't like the idea of writing a letter to God, and even less the idea of getting a letter back, think of this as yet another way of tapping into your unconscious mind. Caroline says it works just as well if you write it to your Higher Self.

The technique is very simple. Get a pad of paper. Sit down and write a letter beginning, 'Dear God'. Then write, without thinking about it too much, whatever situation or problem you'd like help with. Sign it, 'Yours gratefully, [your own name]'.

Now, without stopping to think, write your reply straight back:

Dear [Name],
This is how I see your situation.
This is what I think you should do.
Yours ever,
God

Do not stop to rationalize, consider or criticize. Just keep your hand moving. You'll know when to stop. The answer comes from a wiser, more far-seeing, more compassionate voice, speaking above the stress and panic of daily life. It will surprise you. What it says is personal to you and can be a valuable, ever-present source of advice and encouragement.

As an experiment, because I haven't used this technique for a while, I just stopped to spend time writing a letter to God about a difficult family situation. I was immediately struck by the way in which the need to explain the situation and my own feelings about it to a God-like adviser made me think it through much more clearly and fairly than before. After all, if God doesn't know when you're fudging the issue or being self-justifying, who does? So writing a letter to God in itself encourages the highest level of clarity, understanding and honesty. As I wrote my letter out, fresh solutions were already coming into my mind, but I ploughed on, ignoring them.

When God wrote back, in my own hand (or when I tapped my own deeper understanding and intuition), it was in a spirit of compassion and wisdom. All at once I could see the other person's point of view and how the situation had arisen. I could see what was unchangeable about the problem and how I could behave to avoid getting hurt by it. I even had some fresh and playful ideas about how to introduce a new note, how to get out of the habitual emotional gridlock. God's answer, written uncritically and without pausing to think, gave me fresh perspective, new thinking, renewed compassion, a sense of hope. And a reminder that there's a valuable technique here that I should use more often.

The advantage of writing a letter to God is that you are taking on the voice of an infinitely wise, all-seeing, all-knowing being with the perspective of eternity. There's a spark of that in all of us, and that spark will illuminate your reply.

See also How to Meditate and Why, The Power of Gratitude, The Magic of 20 Minutes, The Freedom of Forgiveness, The Beauty Way

Facing Fear

Twenty years ago I sat in a room listening to a woman describing a course she had been on in North Wales where she found herself at the top of a waterfall looking down into a pool. The course instructor at her side told her to jump. The people below, who had jumped off the waterfall before her, yelled up at her to jump. Her own intellect, which had signed her up for the course in the first place, told her to jump. But something in her argued ferociously back. 'You'll hit your head on a rock and die. The pool isn't deep enough. The pool is too deep – you'll drown. Jump? Never!' And then she jumped.

I felt so sick as she told this story, my stomach churned so sympathetically, my knees felt so weak at the thought of this jump that I just knew, there and then, that I had to go and do the same thing. I wanted to get to the other side of that fear. A year later I found myself trembling on the edge of the waterfall being urged to jump and knowing I couldn't. I couldn't and then – I could. I was under the water and coming up for air.

I wish I could tell you that my life changed on the spot, that, like people walking on a bed of hot coals, I felt mistress of the universe, capable of absolutely anything. I didn't, but I did feel expanded, that I took up more room in the world. I felt more confident and competent. And that day was the end of my resistance to swimming in cold water.

Facing fear is a tale of two powerful emotions. There's the fear itself, which is crippling. And there's the relief and satisfaction on the other side. I was once in Yorkshire at a magical place called Brimham Rocks when two teenage boys were climbing over the giant rock formations. 'Jump!' called one to his timorous friend. 'Go on, jump! It'll make you feel dead hard and cool!'

You can feel dead hard and cool at any age if you get through your own fear barrier. The thing is, fear keeps coming up in front of you. There are always things to be afraid of. Mountaineers get stage fright. Public speakers can be afraid of spiders. Reckless drivers might be afraid of singing in public. Only you know what makes you shrink and say, 'I could never do that.' I may have once jumped off a waterfall, but I'm still afraid of heights and had to sit down on the London Eye.

Each time you give in to a fear you feel a little less good about yourself. A little piece of your confidence is eroded. Each time you overcome a fear you feel a little more dead hard and cool.

Some people can't help setting themselves challenges. As soon as they've conquered one goal they are looking for the next. Other people keep themselves very small by avoiding the feeling of fear at all costs. But sooner or later most of us see something we want, and the very sensation of wanting it is frightening.

We want the promotion, the girl, the prize, so much that we'll go through the fear barrier to get it. And the reward might not be the prize we were after.

The reward might be knowing that we were brave and made an effort and can be brave again.

There is only one question to ask in front of a terrifying challenge: What's the worst that can happen? If the answer is 'I might die or be maimed for life,' then you should certainly pause and at least make sure that you've done the training and are wearing the safety harness. But if it's a loss of ego that scares you, then it is time to face that fear down.

The fear is a very important signal to you that some part of yourself feels under threat. In doing this thing you fear you are going to make yourself vulnerable. You could lose face and be made to look a fool. You could be rejected and be made to feel unlovable. These are horrible things but they are not life-threatening. They are simply part of being alive. They are part of the evolutionary process by which we grow and mature. And as we grow we learn that fear, rather than being a full stop, is simply a signal that something important is going to happen.

See also Made in Error, Saving Yourself from Drowning, The Beauty Way, The Power of Gratitude

Knowing What You Want and Asking for It

Assertiveness training was the very first kind of self-development work I ever did. It happened this way. I didn't wake up one morning and think, *Aha, I must become more assertive.* I just thought, *I need help.*

I was at a stage in my life where I was at home with two children under three and a patchy freelance career, and I somehow felt I had lost the plot. I had no clue what to do about lost plots, but deep down I thought there must be some way of getting perspective on my life or understanding what I was feeling, so I asked my old friend Ann, who also had two children and a career as an artist and was ten years older and wiser than I was.

Ann didn't know what I needed either, but she did know a psychologist and workshop leader whose work she thought was very good. Her name was Anne Dickson and when I rang her up she was about to start teaching an eight-week course of assertiveness training, and that is how I found myself, for the first time in my life, sitting with a group of strangers being given the behavioural tools to work out what I wanted in life and, crucially, how to get it without being aggressive, whiney, manipulative or self-defeating.

Assertiveness training turned out to be about clarity and honesty, and the day came, much more quickly than I expected, when I put it into practice and it worked.

Anyone who has small children knows how difficult it can be to work at home. I wanted to be my independent working self and I wanted to earn money and I also wanted to be with my children. My husband thought I'd be much happier if I got out of the house and took a full-time job and made the whole thing organized and clear-cut, but I wasn't ready for that. I felt I wanted some kind of relationship with an employer that gave me regular work but didn't take all my time. I fixed myself an interview with a former employer, *The Sunday Times*, to see if they had shift work on the news desk.

As I walked the streets between my house and *The Sunday Times'* office my assertively trained brain began to think about the interview, and this is what I thought: *If you're not careful, you are going to get yourself in deep trouble. News is irregular and out of normal hours. You're going to offer your services and you could end up being at the beck and call of a news desk with no fixed limits, which will make it impossible to plan your time or childcare. There's no point going in there and just saying you'd love to work for them, because you wouldn't. You've got to be clearer than that.* And then this new crisp voice came into my head and said, 'What you want is to go and work on the news desk for two days a week. That would be perfect. You'd get enough money and stimulation and experience and you'd get to spend the rest of your time at home.'

Half an hour later I sat in the news editor's office and found myself saying, 'What I'd really like is to come in and work on the news desk two days a week.'

'Fine,' he said, just like that. 'When could you start?'

I was astonished, though I didn't show it. That week I was able to bounce into my assertiveness training class and say, 'Guess what? This stuff really works.'

That was nearly 20 years ago and I've found the techniques of assertiveness training useful ever since. Whether you're negotiating a job, navigating a sticky patch in a relationship or returning shoddy goods to a shop, it's a great tool for being honest with yourself and clear with other people.

See also Is It Ever Too Late to Change? The Art of Self-reinvention, The Power of Gratitude, The Freedom of Forgiveness

How to Be Creative

There are thousands of people who dream of being artists and writers, people who write secretly and tear up their writing, people who paint but don't dare show their paintings to anyone. Sometimes I hear from them and sometimes I meet them and, if they ask my advice, this is what I say:

'If I were the Wizard of Oz I would recognize your problem as lack of artistic courage and I would hand you some kind of gold medal that would make your chest swell with pride and give you the self-confidence to get out there and make mistakes.'

Notice I didn't say, 'Get out there and sell your work.' I don't think this is the problem. I think the problem is that thousands of people with some creative ability have quite unrealistic ideas of what making art involves. So this life lesson is for everyone who tells bedtime stories to their grandchildren and dreams of being J K Rowling, or who painted some nice pictures on holiday and wonders if they could sell them.

A) There is a whole lot more to the artistic life than that and B) if you could let go of the idea of an end-product and commit yourself to the never-ending process of creative exploration you would have the basis of a very rich life. And, maybe, as a by-product, you might produce something worth selling, but that isn't really the point. The point is to experiment and improve and make your own discoveries.

I remember when I was doing an adult education art course and my daughter was keen to know how I was getting on. Was my work good? Did the teacher give it good marks? Was I top of the class? I tried to explain that learning art didn't really work like that beyond school. Nobody ever told you your work was good. They used open-ended words like 'interesting' and 'promising'. What they inevitably said, until you learned to incorporate the question so that it didn't need asking, was, 'And how are you going to take it further?'

Taking it further meant anything from scaling it up or down to cutting it up in pieces and setting fire to it. The essential lesson is that, as soon as you are precious and possessive about something you have done, you might as well wrap it up and take it home and sit on it – which is what many would-be artists do.

I just dug up an interview I did with the artist brothers Jake and Dinos Chapman, who stand about as far away from this approach to art as it is possible to be. Nevertheless, they have something to teach. Dinos said, 'Art is deeply unsatisfactory. If making something made you feel deeply satisfied you wouldn't feel the necessity to make another one. We're plagued by demons. What we make is a trail of gravestones.'

Now a gravestone by Jake and Dinos Chapman would be worth a lot of money, but that is because, whatever you think of it, their work is alive. It is the record of an ongoing self-discipline and inquiry that makes it interesting and demonstrates to the world that they take their art very seriously. By feeling too timid to show anybody, even the people you invite into your home, what you do, you demonstrate that you are not really taking it very seriously, however much you say your work is like your own children.

Worst of all, I don't think you are getting a fraction of the interest and excitement out of it that I think you could if you were more ruthless with yourself and a lot braver.

So what can you do? If you are stuck – and what artist doesn't get stuck? – I suggest you start looking outside yourself and finding where in the world your work might fit in. Go to exhibitions, museums, craft fairs, art galleries. Look in libraries and bookshops. What excites you and inspires you? Who can you steal from? I'm serious. Be a magpie. Go back to your own work with your new inspiration and knowledge and think how you might change it. What avenues would you like to explore? What colours and techniques would you like to try?

Someone careful and controlled and timid is likely to lose their nerve at this point. Instead of being inspired by all the work they've seen, they are vulnerable to a draining of self-confidence. This is why I strongly suggest to anyone who wants to develop their creativity that they get out of their solitary space and find a congenial class, any class – painting, sculpture, watercolour, weaving. Get back to art school. Join a writing group. Get among your peers and breathe a common air of shared endeavour. It will galvanize you into fresh enthusiasm and you will get more honest reaction from a good teacher and from fellow students than you will from your friends, who may well like your work but are also afraid of hurting your sensitive feelings with any adverse criticism.

As well as the steps above, I recommend, for frustrated, isolated artists everywhere, Julia Cameron's book *The Artist's Way*. Now you are not on your own any more. You are at the beginning of a whole new phase of creativity.

If you get stuck again, I share with you a quotation I heard from an African woman whose tribe made houses beautifully decorated in coloured mud.

The walls needed constantly redecorating, and visiting tourists sighed at the waste of so much creativity. Why didn't the women put this work into pictures they could hang on the walls? 'They have their little forevers,' laughed the village women, 'but we are forever creating.' Learn from them.

There is no art without risk, and life is in the process, not the product.

See also Made in Error, The Magic of 20 Minutes, A Short Guide to the Subconscious, The Beauty Way

The Magic of 20 Minutes

When people learn that I wrote a book about everything I've ever done that worked, they are puzzled and polite. I try to explain that it's not about how to unblock the sink, more about how to unblock themselves. If you were really stuck in a place you didn't like – a bad relationship, an unfulfilling job, a work crisis, a creative impasse, an emotional loop – and something in this book got you unstuck and flowing, I would call that a result.

When people hear this, they go a bit quiet. Then they might say, 'Have you got anything about being blocked?' Or 'Have you got anything to help creativity?' Or 'My biggest problem is focus.' Or 'I'm so overloaded, I could cry at any minute.' To all of them I would say, 'Yes, I know a trick or two that can help. Try writing a letter to God, try expressing gratitude, even when you're feeling overwhelmed by fear. Try being your own best friend. Above all, try pulling focus: get very, very small. Get as small as 20 minutes.'

When I feel stuck or unfocused or miserable, everything feels huge and insurmountable. The problem I'm blocked on seems overwhelming and too big to tackle. And what this makes me feel is that I can't, and don't, want to do it at all. My resistance is huge, so I'll put it off till tomorrow or some time when I feel like it. That's what 'procrastination' means, by the way. *Pro cras*. For tomorrow. And we all know when tomorrow comes – never. Which is why the problem doesn't get solved, the focus doesn't get pulled, the great creative breakthrough doesn't happen, ever.

What works is to do the smallest possible thing you can contemplate doing. Can you sit down and write a symphony? No. Can you write a movement? No. Could you write a few bars, 20 minutes' worth? Could you sit at your piano or your music paper for 20 minutes, undistracted by fear, self-criticism, other tasks? It's only 20 minutes. Yes, you could do that. And having done that you might find you could manage five minutes more. And so on.

Never underestimate the power of inertia. It takes far more energy and fuel for a plane to take off than it does to cruise. Cruising is the easy bit. That's why the kind of people who finish projects have many ways to get themselves onto the runway and taxiing off. Some writers finish work in the middle of a sentence so that they can start again the next morning. Some begin by writing their own name over and over until their hand and brain start to write something more interesting.

Above all, you have to stay where you are. Artists go into their studios and stay there, pottering, going through the motions, until something clicks in and ideas begin to work. It might take all day for an original idea to happen, but the action of turning up in the studio or at the desk and staying there lets your unconscious know that you're serious. It's like unblocking a sink, after all. Nothing happens and nothing happens, but you keep trying and then, with a glug and a burp, things start moving. And it's the small things, the increments of 20 minutes, that can bring the shift.

Journalism taught me that the breakthrough often comes with the one extra phone call you don't feel like making. You're getting nowhere and you want to give up and then the last question in the interview gives you the extra insight, the one great quote you've been waiting for. Art training taught me that the creative solution or original idea comes when you're tired and working, not when you are planning a project from the outside. Somehow, if you stick with the work, you reach a point where your controlling mind lets go and a fresh connection sparks. It often happens when I say to myself, 'I'll just do another 20 minutes.'

Whatever it is, you have to be there, with your attention focused. Even, let's say, if you're in the biggest emotional mess and you don't know where to turn or how to think, allow yourself to really feel, really express, sob, howl, rage for 20 minutes and you may find that 20 minutes will take you through to a temporary calm, a small clearing where you can begin to think straight. And after that, another five, another 20 ...

It's about leverage. Archimedes said that if he had a place to stand he could move the world. In a tumultuous, frustrating, intransigent world, 20 minutes is our place to stand.

See also Stepping Stones, My Samurai Partner, Knowing What You Want and Asking for It, A Short Guide to the Subconscious

Make Friends with Money

Money and sex are the two issues we find it hardest to talk about, the two issues that break up the most marriages. Which is the bigger taboo? Which is hardly ever taught in schools? Which gives you the bigger jolt of fear on a regular basis? Which are you more likely to lie awake worrying about? Which are you most willing to sweep under the carpet or leave to somebody else to take care of? Which produces the most sense of panic and helplessness? Yes, it's not sex. It's money.

It works to make friends with money. It's going to be your daily concern for the whole of your life, so it doesn't make sense to ignore it or leave it to other people. Even at the start of your working career there are ways to budget, to manage your debts, to organize your savings, to work out how much you need to spend and how much to put aside for the future. Above all, you need to know how to avoid expensive debts.

I'm not going to go into all of this here, because there are plenty of good books about basic financial management. There are excellent money sections in the newspapers aimed at ordinary people with ordinary lives and ordinary incomes. There are agencies, like the Citizens Advice Bureau, which can help you restructure loan repayments. There are independent financial advisors who are not in the pay of institutions and who are bound to disclose what commission they get on selling you financial products. Beware of advice from institutions, like banks, which have a vested interest in selling you their own products. Their advice is not disinterested. Money is their business and they make it on the loans and products they persuade you to take out.

Taking charge of your money – knowing where it is coming from, where it is going and exactly what you are spending and saving – is hugely important for your sense of independence and self-worth. It doesn't matter who you are, how you see yourself, how unworldly and non-materialistic you want to be, you can't get away with ignoring it. I've observed that those people who think they are above and beyond money are usually very reliant on other people's. Don't be like that. It's just not grown up and it loses you friends.

Getting in a muddle and losing control of your finances can lead to dread, confusion and despair. Never ignore a financial problem, because it will grow in the dark. The sooner you admit to it and communicate with the relevant people, the easier it is to resolve. Non-communication drives financial institutions mad and they will penalize you even more heavily.

If your money is in a muddle, the only way to start gaining control of it is with a day of reckoning. Start by honestly keeping an account of everything you spend, day by day. You'll soon see where the money is going. And go through your bank statements, item by item. You may be one of those people who would rather earn more than spend less, but unless you keep an account of your getting and spending, how will you ever know where to begin?

Your relationship with money is one of the most important in your life and, as with all relationships, truth is the only basis that works.

And, as a rule of thumb, it's always better to make it than take it.

See also The Research and Development Fund, My Samurai Partner, Writing a Letter to God

Stepping Stones

I have made my way through life on stepping stones. This isn't the only way. Look around and you will see that people build their lives very differently. Some hack their way through the jungle, slashing and burning and transforming the landscape. Some are always taking wild leaps into the dark. Sometimes they land on their feet. Sometimes they miss and fall. Some people are so paralysed by the risks inherent in change that they crouch in the undergrowth for years, becoming more entrenched as time passes them by. Some are full of wild schemes that they never try out. Some waste years longing to be rescued. When it comes to making changes in life I have found that stepping stones work for me.

Using stepping stones as your method of forward motion means that you never make a leap without having a landing place. It may not be dry land. It may not be a settled resting place, but it will be movement in the direction in which you wish to travel.

What do stepping stones look like? A stepping stone towards the change you really want will not be the change in its entirety. So if it's a dream job you are after it won't be the dream job, but neither will the stone you are leaving behind. Stepping stones are the stages that will get you there when the distance between where you stand and where you want to be is too great to cross in one leap.

You create stepping stones by doing research and making connections. Say you are after that dream job. You can't get it straight away, so you consider training and voluntary work. You offer to do unpaid work if it will get you nearer your goal. You read articles that name people who do the kind of work you want or who could help you, and you write to these people asking for their advice and if you could maybe even meet them. They can only say 'no' or, more usually, not reply at all. But one 'yes' could make all the difference.

Even moving via stepping stones means taking risks – the risk of putting your ideas out into the open and looking foolish – but you must do that if you are to make change.

So you start moving in your chosen direction, stepping stone by stepping stone. If you want to make films, you get a camera and start making something you can show to other people. If you want to write, you start writing and join a writing group. If you want to make political change, you go to meetings and demonstrations and join lobby groups. You volunteer. You meet like-minded people and one thing leads to another.

Stepping stones are not just about finding a new job. They can be moves towards the kind of life you really want to live. Have you thought of moving abroad? Go on holiday to another country and do a recce. Do you feel you've outgrown your friends? Get involved with an activity that attracts you and you will meet like-minded people. Do you long to move to a different part of town? Stop fantasizing about it and start walking round new neighbourhoods. Consider renting while you look. Life doesn't have to be all or nothing with no safety net. It can be trial and error.

Making your way on stepping stones means building on the great truth that one thing leads to another. And one person leads to another. When you make your intention known to the people you meet in the gym or in your terrible job or at your local party meeting, somebody may say that their friend's aunt or their neighbour's cousin knows somebody who knows something about what you want. Always follow up leads. Every lead is a stepping stone. And one stone leads to another.

If you have ever tried to cross a stream by creating your own stepping stone you will know that it can be a hit-or-miss business. The stone you are trying to position ahead of yourself disappears under the water. Or it is insecure and wobbles wildly when you try to step on it. This doesn't matter. Cast about for more stones and just keep chucking them into the water. Sooner or later you will create a firm footing.

The other crucial point about stepping stones is that you never step off the one you are on until the next one is in place and will take your weight. I once made the mistake of giving up one job before I had secured the next. You recover, of course, but you have made life harder for yourself. Waist-deep in flowing water is not an easy base from which to make a change. Even the smallest stone, the least promising job, the least likely contact, is a springboard to the next.

One day you will step onto a stone which leads to dry land. Congratulations. You've made it across. All those letters and emails, all those contacts, all that research, all that unpaid preparation, lobbying and persistence have carried you through to the place where you wanted to be.

Do you still want to be there? Or has your mind leaped ahead to a new destination across another wide stretch of water? It doesn't matter now, because you've learned the art of getting there. Stepping stones will get you anywhere you want to go.

See also The Research and Development Fund, The Art of Self-reinvention, The Magic of 20 Minutes, Is It Ever Too Late to Change?

Who Should I Be Doing It With?

Or, if you must, with whom should I be? 'Who?' is the fundamental question. Who will I find to love me? Who will I marry? To whom am I important? To whom do I owe any duty? For whom must I care? Who will stand by me? And if I find a 'who', be it friend, colleague or lover, how do I make this work?

It's not just about love – at least, not the romantic kind. Other people bring us the greatest ecstasy, cause us the most profound pain. We are still learning about the intricacies of relationships with others until the day we die. I wrote a whole book to try to fathom the complexities of the ways in which we need each other. The following pieces touch on some of the ways in which we can create richer relationships and understand and improve our relationships with others, beginning with an account of my own parents' 60-year-long marriage.

How to Stay Married for 60 Years

We were planning a special lunch for my parents' diamond wedding anniversary in a lovely country hotel. My 84-year-old father and I had gone in to view the room, pick the champagne, choose the food. Then my mother fell ill and went into hospital, so the event was postponed.

On the eve of the anniversary my father rang me at half past ten at night. 'I've been thinking,' he said, 'that tomorrow I will have been married to your mother for 60 years, and it seems quite wrong to go and visit her in hospital in the afternoon as if it were just a normal day. I want to get up and go straight there in a taxi first thing in the morning. What do you think?'

'Quite right,' I said, even though, for the last six months, my father had been housebound with the multiple afflictions of the elderly, and spent most of his mornings in bed. 'It's time for a grand romantic gesture.'

And so my father, who is rarely up and fully dressed before noon, rose, washed, shaved and dressed before nine o'clock. He then set off in a taxi to the hospital, where my 81-year-old mother was marooned with pancreatitis. There he told her, in the setting of a public ward, for the umpteen thousandth time, how much he loved her.

On the brilliant May day on which they married in an English country church 60 years before, my giddy, exuberant young parents had known each other for less than six weeks. It was wartime, 1944, and he was a 24-year-old flight lieutenant in the RAF and she was a young member of the WAAF. He fell for her as soon as he saw 'this delicious little thing'. A day later he asked her to marry him and she laid her head on his chest and said, 'Thank you very much, but no.' A couple of weeks of persistence, poetry and relentless charm later she said, 'Ask me again.' So he did and she said yes. When he asked her why she'd changed her mind she said, 'You're good looking, you're clever and you've got a good degree and I'm a bit of an intellectual snob.' They were married a week later by special licence from the Bishop of Salisbury. Well, it was wartime.

There was no time to meet each other's families, although my uncle got leave from the army long enough to give my mother away. My father was married in his uniform and my mother in a smart little suit, and their honeymoon night was spent in a nearby seaside hotel.

On the day of their diamond wedding anniversary, 60 years later, the weather was just as glorious as it had been all that time ago. When I took my father back to my mother's hospital ward that afternoon, we carried cards and presents and a cake and an aromatic posy of flowers. We sat outside the ward in a sunny courtyard and wondered how it was they'd stayed together all these years.

My father, who is a writer whose hands have become disablingly crippled with arthritis, had begun his day by opening his long-abandoned journal. 'On this day, 60 years ago,' he wrote, in his arthritic spidery writing, 'I had the great good fortune to be married to Wendy.' When I said, 'Go on, Dad, what's the secret?' he thought for a second and then said emphatically, 'Luck.'

Well, there is an element of luck in marrying somebody you've only known for six weeks and finding out, over sixty long years, that you haven't married an axe-murderer, but someone infinitely loving, good and kind. My mother, naturally, thought there was more to it than that. "It's never considering that there's an alternative," she said. "It's being able to be very cross with each other but never falling out," said my dad. "And always having interesting things of your own to do so you're not just dependent on each other," added my mother.

All of these things are true. I have my own point of view, the unique and privileged view of an only child. In this triumvirate I am the perpetual witness and also often the recipient of both the loving and the critical confidences of each parent about the other.

"Your father is a very trying man," sighs my mother, but she is still lovingly willing to be tried. "Your mother is very impetuous and headstrong," grumbles my father, and goes on to mutter that, although everyone thinks my mother is sweet and saintly, she actually has a very nasty temper, which I know is true.

And they confide the good things too. "Your father is a very remarkable man," says my mother. "Your mother is a very good kind person," says my father, who is much less forgiving and sociably inclusive than she is.

Sometimes, as the recipient of a moment of exasperation or frustration, I have made the great mistake of trying to act as the advocate for the temporarily disgruntled one. But it only serves to have them unite against me. I will be told that nobody is as close as they are, nobody more lovingly partnered, that if I think either one of them is being unkind or inconsiderate to the other then I don't understand the unique nature of their relationship. I shut up.

This is what I observe, as the sole product and lifelong witness of this uniquely close and constantly lively partnership. It is a relationship where there are few moments of silence. These two people find each other constantly interesting. They talk continuously, about the state of the world, about what they are reading or watching on television, about what they should eat for dinner or plant in the garden. They enliven this non-stop dialogue by bickering and arguing, but are upset if anyone should mistake this sparring for a genuine row.

They disagree constantly. They each have a great respect for the other, but they each also have a great respect for themselves and their opinions, and defend them vigorously. They also love each other very much, and their most heated arguments take place when one is convinced that they know exactly what is best for the other.

There is a tidal flow to this constant, uninterrupted interchange. Sometimes it is heated argument and barbed frustration. Sometimes it is quiet and tender, and expresses itself in a soft kiss, a hug or a gentle pat on the hand or cheek. My mother tries to remove the obstacles from my father's path. My father tries to rein my mother in and stop her from over-running or exhausting herself. When either one is down, the other quivers with sympathetic anxiety. In moments of relaxation or holiday they are still quintessentially youthful. In their eighties, they still have an intellectual brightness, a vivacity, a humour that made them irresistible when they were young, vigorous, good looking and full of bounce.

There have been difficult and trying times in my parents' lives, periods of crisis and illness and drama. But neither of them ever gives up, not on life, not on the problem, not on each other. They are good at remembering to appreciate each other. My mother always looks immaculate and wonderful, and my father is always proud that she does. My mother is often dumbstruck by my father's ingenuity, resourcefulness and sheer brain power.

Some battles they will never win. My father says that in sixty years my mother has never let him finish a sentence. My father, over sixty years which must mean at least twenty thousand dinners, has never failed to drive my mother demented by disappearing somewhere just as the hot food is set on the table. But he also never fails to appreciate the food and tell her how good it is. I have seen my mother fly at my father in 5 foot of unleashed fury, and I have seen my father draw himself up to his full 6 feet and say, his voice tight with resentment, that he will never forgive her for whichever affront she has committed. But she calms down and he does forgive her. Nothing is irrevocable, the sweetness always returns.

My daughter, their granddaughter, says that my mother told her that they had been through plenty of things that other people might have got divorced over, but they never did. "It's a shame," says my daughter, "when you look at all the people who get divorced and who won't ever know what it's like to be together for so long."

What is it like? It is to be half of a lifelong dialogue. It is to be quite separate, strong-willed, highly individual people whose utter commitment to each other, through weariness, rage, despair, intense irritation, illness, breakdown, is completely non-negotiable. I can't imagine they have ever wasted a minute talking about whether to separate, although they may have spent hours, days, talking about how to get through the next stage together. It is to be two opposing poles, forever repelled, forever drawn to each other. It is to be two people more stricken by anxiety for the other than by thought for themselves. It is to be two people who would never, ever let the other down, say goodnight without tenderness, or leave without a parting kiss. It is to be two people fiercely driven by what is right for the other. It is to be two people in an indivisible, impenetrable whole. And it is to be two people who are an endlessly renewable source of loving care and forgiveness for each other.

It has been some years since my father admitted to me that they had reached the stage of life where they each wake in the morning and listen to hear if the other is still breathing. The angel of death has hovered around a few times, darkening our lives with the shadow of fatal wings, before flapping off again without landing this time. I strongly suspect that he found my parents, even in age and sickness, too deep in their sixty-year-long exchange of challenge, care and concern to pay him the right sort of attention.

See also The Power of Gratitude, Set Your Compass to Love, Making a Life with Meaning

Relating to the World

Ever since I came back from an Ayurvedic resort in Sri Lanka where I detoxed my body and mind, I have been keeping a log of my daily habits. One of the items on the log, along with food and exercise, is 'Relationships'.

'Relationships' is a much-abused word. We use it geographically, like a place to be, as in, 'Are you in a relationship?' We use it as an object of desire, as in, 'I'm looking for the perfect relationship.' And we treat it as a fragile object, as in, 'My relationship's just broken up.' What we clearly mean, in all these usages, is a relationship with one significant other.

That's not what I mean when I write my daily log book. I mean relationships with any other human being. Keeping a record has made me redefine and revalue what relationships are, what they mean to me and, indeed, what part they play in the business of being human. Just checking the log I see that dinner with my ex-husband or a weekend with my cousins are part of my relationship web, but so are the long phone calls with friends, the conversation I had with my hairdresser or the masseuse, the exchange in a business meeting or the chat I had on the pavement with a neighbour. The emotional intensity may be different, but each one is a reconnect, a plug-in to the larger community. And each contact revives, renews and redefines me. In putting each encounter into my daily log I am giving all these smaller relationships a higher value.

We put so much emphasis on the One True Significant Relationship that we overlook the infinitely rich sea of other relationships in which we swim.

What I love about this supporting cast of relationships is that it is always available. Unlike the One, who might come along once in a lifetime, the Many are always swimming about there in shoals, just waiting to be noticed, engaged and nourished in their turn.

Once you see that you have a relationship with the world and not just with a dream, then every encounter becomes a potential for a real exchange. You can make it a challenge to get a smile out of the grumpy newspaper vendor or to call the checkout girl by her name, since she has it on a tag on her lapel.

If you really want to expand your relationship with the world, you can think even bigger than the daily casual encounters. You can make things happen. A couple of my neighbours rang up the other week because they'd been invited to a neighbourhood party for the people on their street and wanted me to come along. Two extremely enterprising young people had taken it upon themselves to throw a 'Meet the Neighbours' party in a local bar. They had pushed 500 invitations through every door in the nearby network of streets, counting on getting a 25 per cent take-up rate. Everyone who turned up thought the idea was brilliant. Names and numbers were exchanged, familiar faces had names attached. Local concerns and local gossip were swapped.

It is crucially important to cultivate relationships in the plural even when you are in a relationship with the One, because any exclusive relationship can go wrong and then you need the rest of the world more than ever. I wrote a piece one Valentine's Day – asked for, very tactfully, by an editor who knew my marriage had broken up and who wondered, very nicely, if I felt like writing a piece about being alone on Valentine's Day. I took a big gulp and then, on behalf of the thousands, millions, of other people who were also alone on Valentine's Day, said I would.

It cheered me up a lot writing that piece because, perhaps for the first time, it made me look at the ways in which my life, post-separation, had actually become richer. I had begun singing in a choir. I had made friends, male and female, through music who had brought a whole new dimension into my life and filled my diary too. I had had fun of a simple, uncomplicated kind that I hadn't had for years. When it was published I had cheering mail from other singles who had also found that, post the break-up, there is more than safety in numbers, there is joy too. There are new friends, surprising opportunities and new beginnings. A happy side-effect of this can be that the

inevitable bitterness and blame of break-ups are eased and the broken relationship with the One can become, in time, another friendship.

Which is why, when I look back at the moments of heartache in my life I can see, with the clarity of distance, that there is a hidden blessing in each experience of loss. The end of each exclusive relationship has opened the door to the rediscovery of old friends and, always, the making of some new ones. Sometimes, in the light of these new relationships, we can see that maybe we hung on to the old one for too long, simply because we were afraid of a void which, now we are there, is no void at all. In fact, if you take the heat off looking for the One, look the world in the eye and smile at it, there is never a void.

See also Singles and Their Habitat, The Power of the People, The Power of Gratitude

Singles and Their Habitat

When you are young and surrounded by people your own age, potential partners are everywhere. Later on you have to work harder. In the interests of research for this book, I took myself off to a weekend workshop on relationships run by Seana McGee and Maurice Taylor, authors of *The New Couple*. It was for singles, and I had worked out before I went that the girls would outnumber the men by quite a lot, though the workshops are for both sexes and men do go. I have learned from experience that most British men would rather have root-canal work done than spend more than five minutes talking about relationships and emotions. When I found that this workshop coincided with a major football match, then I didn't expect to see any men at all – and I was right.

But the other girls on the workshop were disappointed. They thought they might meet someone. Well, we all learned a lot about how to make relationships work that weekend. We learned about anger and how to express it healthily. We learned how to listen, and we learned how to value ourselves so highly that we could set conditions for our future relationships. If you want to know more about what we learned, I suggest you get Seana and Maurice's book. What we didn't really learn, although it was what concerned us all, was where to find our future soul mates.

If you are a man, you need to know that there were 25 women there that weekend, all attractive, all bright, all available. Wouldn't it have been worth giving up a weekend of your time for an opportunity like that? Especially as these women were learning some skills that could prevent a lot of grief in any future relationship. And if not that particular workshop, well, any other workshop would do. The world of personal development is a world where women always seem to outnumber men.

If you are a woman looking for a man, you could learn from Rosie, who was also on this workshop and said she often meets men playing golf, although she met her latest date through work. And I bet that, if you could have attracted their attention, there were plenty of men at that major football match. If you are going to find fault with this line of thinking, you could argue that you don't want to date the kind of girl who hangs out in personal growth workshops, nor do you want the kind of man who spends his time playing or watching sport. But women are interested in emotions and are more open to self-improvement than men, just as more men are interested in sport – of course there are plenty that aren't, but we're talking averages here. It wasn't because I loved cricket that I volunteered to make the teas at cricket matches when I was at school. It was because I was interested in boys, and there they were. And there they still are, decades later.

Once you are out of higher education and into a world limited by workplaces and working hours, it becomes a lot more difficult to find people to love. Internet chatlines and dating services have mushroomed to serve generations of single people who are chained to their computers. It seems there is a higher chance of meeting somebody in cyberspace than there is of meeting a real, available person in a local bar or at a party. After all, there are millions of people out there in cyberspace, and there are the same old people you already know at your local bar.

Nevertheless, for your own sense of self-worth and amusement, and for increasing your chances of meeting somebody you like, the old advice still applies. Just get out more. I had a very entertaining day recently when I went to the races. There were lots of amusing men, and I came home slightly better off than I went. I was at an art gallery opening last night and it was packed with single people in their twenties and thirties. A year's membership to the art gallery guarantees me a lot of invitations like that, and I get to learn a lot more about art, which improves my whole quality of life. I didn't meet anybody to love at the opening, but I did go home in a really good mood.

Everyone has to eat, so bars and restaurants and supermarkets are on most people's trajectory. And everyone has to work. The workplace, both statistically and in my experience, is where most people meet, which is why I'm a bit baffled by efforts to cut down romance in the workplace. If not there, then where? And if you want to up your chances, try to find a job in a place where there are plenty of members of the opposite sex. For example, as a young journalist I learned fast that the offices of women's magazines are full of women, whereas newspapers have far more men around. Simple really. If you're a woman, work on a newspaper. If you're a man, try women's magazines.

The secret of happiness, though, is to think bigger than the desperate search to find somebody. You have to do things you enjoy. You have to do things that improve your quality of life, whether or not you are sharing it with anybody. And if your enjoyable life leads you to a partner, that's a bonus.

See also The Power of Gratitude, Being Your Own Best Friend, Knowing What You Want and Asking for It, Set Your Compass to Love

My Samurai Partner

Marianna is my Samurai partner. A Samurai partner is a friend, but more than a friend. It is a friend with rules and parameters attached, and when you are contemplating change in your life or struggling with change that is happening to you, a Samurai partner is a very precious thing.

I can't remember exactly how Marianna and I fell into this relationship, but we were already friends and we had ambitions and organized minds, and Marianna had once gone on a course called Samurai, which involved getting up at dawn and changing your life. Part of the Samurai strategy was to have a buddy to meet up with regularly so you could keep each other on track. I don't know what happened to Marianna's previous Samurai partner, but I became her new one. At a tumultuous time in both our lives when we were full of dreams and obstacles to those dreams, we would meet, notebooks and pens in hand, and we would analyse and we would envision and we would plan.

The essence of a Samurai partnership is equal listening. It's not like an everyday friendship where two people will get together over a drink or a coffee. Then one will let off steam and the other will nod and grunt and, as soon as there is a gap in the conversation, will throw in their two penn'orth of gratuitous advice or, more likely, say, 'That's exactly like this thing that's happened to me,' and go off on a rant of their own while friend number one waits patiently for the chance to bring the conversation round their way again. Of course this kind of friendship is therapeutic and vital, but a Samurai partnership isn't like that. Samurai partnerships get things done.

At the beginning of a Samurai session you both decide how long you want to speak for, and when you have decided whether you want 15 minutes or half an hour or an hour each, you decide who goes first. The role of the listening partner is to be wholly attentive to the one who talks. This is not the time for personal experiences of your own – that can come later. Your job is to pay extreme attention, ask elucidating questions, maybe make notes. You may spot inconsistencies and have useful suggestions. Your aim is to help the other person arrive at a plan of action, preferably one to be executed in manageable stages and within a realistic time frame, all of which you write down. When the allotted time is up, you stop. You can always return to tidy up the loose ends once the second person has taken their turn at talking through their situation.

As I remember it, when Marianna and I first started working together she was thinking of going to live abroad and my marriage was falling apart. We came at our problems from all kinds of angles. We spent time drawing up a five-year plan and a two-year plan that covered all areas of our lives. By the time we left each session we had an action list to be carried out before we met again in a week's or two weeks' time.

The basis of this relationship was trust and somehow that the two of us were on the same wavelength at the time. We were also both energetic and efficient. We both had blank spots which were easier for the other one to see. I think we also genuinely wanted the best for each other. We wanted to see each other fulfilled and happy.

That was 15 years ago now. Marianna went off to live in Greece and we haven't had a Samurai session in years, but I valued them and I still value her friendship and I would recommend a Samurai relationship to anybody. Life coaches charge an awful lot of money, though they are disinterested and they have professional skills of their own to apply. But if you are not in complete confusion and if you are genuinely committed to making changes and you find a like-minded buddy, team up. It can be a special relationship. I have a number of good friends I confide in, but only one Samurai partner.

See also Writing a Letter to God, The Magic of 20 Minutes, The Power of the People, The Art of Self-reinvention

The Power of the People

There are two great delusions about changing the world. One is that you are a martyr because you have to do everything on your own. The other is that you are a hero because you have to do everything on your own. The first one gets more of a grip as you get older and gloomier. The second one is a fantasy of youth and is much more fun.

Who hasn't dreamed about being a superhero who single-handedly saves the world? Ours is the struggle, true, but ours are the glory and the adulation, which, of course, we shrug off modestly before going back to our humble ways. Harry Potter, Frodo, Superman, Pippi Longstocking, Wonder Woman – the saviour has many names and many shapes. Why not us? It could happen. People and animals and supernatural beings could appear to give us a helping hand, but in the darkest hours we could be the ones who single-handedly face down the forces of evil.

All this gets a bit tiring as you pass adolescence. It turns out that we don't have the power to save the world single-handedly and, worse, it takes all the power we have just to get to work on time or get our children to do their homework. We may worry about pollution and the war on terror, but there's not much energy over at the end of the day to do much about it. It turns out we aren't Superman or Superwoman after all. And if we're not careful, we find ourselves turning to the martyr fantasy and groaning under the burden of having to do everything on our own. Only we don't.

Solitary struggle is a bit of an indulgence. Whatever it is you are trying to do, there are people out there who can help lighten the load, spread the message, rally the troops and save the world. Every movement, whether in politics or art or philosophy, began with a handful of people who found they thought the same way. Every difficult human situation, whether it is solitary confinement, caring for the elderly, mental illness or single parenthood, has attracted support organizations and campaigners, pathfinders who have been there before and helpers who will give encouragement.

When it comes to changing the world in a big way, there is so much more momentum in a movement than in a single human being. I don't know what you care about, but I am sure you care about something. It might be arresting the pace of climate change. It might be global justice. It might be workers' rights or regeneration through art. It might be conserving threatened buildings or re-routing roads or challenging the dominance of supermarkets. Whatever it is, I promise you that, no matter where you live, there are other people who think and feel as you do.

When you find those people, you will be so much more effective and your life will be much richer. Where do you find them? Everywhere. You find them through your passions. You find them through the Internet, through political organizations, in centres of education and learning, in pressure groups and charities, on evening classes and courses, in the pages of publications that report on the topics that interest you most. You meet them at your children's school gate or among your neighbours when you start a petition.

The benefits of bonding with other people come at every level and I wouldn't place political action above the life-enhancing plus of friendship. I know what it is to feel lonely and isolated and excluded, but when I challenge myself on it I admit that this is an illusion which I can dispel just as soon as I walk onto the street or pick up the phone. Solitude is valuable, but we evolved to be social and joining in doesn't just prolong our life (which it does), it makes it worth living.

See also My Samurai Partner, Making a Life with Meaning, Writing a Letter to God, Relating to the World

When You Want to Help Somebody Else

I once attended a Buddhist retreat at Samye Ling in Scotland, where a venerable Tibetan lama was holding a question-and-answer session. A rather cross woman attacked him for his advice to a woman on the previous day. The woman had a husband who was violent and beat her, and the lama's advice to her was to get out of her husband's way.

'This isn't good enough,' said the cross woman. 'We would think that the man ought to seek help for his violent behaviour and deal with his own issues and not take them out on his wife.'

The venerable lama nodded and smiled as the translator explained the question. Then he gave his answer back. 'What you say is perfectly true,' he said. 'And if the man were standing in front of me I would tell him to seek help for his violent behaviour and to deal with his issues and not take them out on his wife. But it is not the man, but the woman, who asked me for help. And to the woman I say, get out of the way.'

As soon as I opened shop to people and their problems I realized that much of the unhappiness we suffer is over somebody else. We helplessly witness a friend's brutal marriage. Teenagers worry about separating parents. Parents are distressed by their children's struggles. It is good that we care about others and it is good that others care about us. Otherwise life would be intolerable. Nevertheless, there is a limit to what we can do, and each time I hear from somebody who longs to set somebody else's life straight, I remember that wise Tibetan lama.

You see, if somebody writes to me about a loved one's difficult marriage, it is not she nor even her allegedly cruel husband who has written to me. It is a relative. The relative is not part of this relationship. The rest of the family have the common and unenviable role of standing to one side and longing to intervene but feeling powerless. And they can feel worse than powerless. Their own health and happiness can be dragged down by the perceived needs of others. If this is you, I am not telling you to get out of the way exactly, but you have no choice but to stay out of the way until the protagonists ask for your help.

Quite a number of people write to me because they are seriously concerned about a son or daughter, a sister or brother. They want to know what they can do to sort this person's life out, and I can sympathize. It is horrible to be the impotent witness to what looks like an impending car crash. From the dungheap of one's own unresolved issues and unsatisfactory relationships, it is easy to have a bird's-eye view of someone else's problems and how they can be sorted.

In the light of my experience I can only say that your bird's-eye view may not be their view at all. While you are lying sleeplessly in bed at night, they may be suffering but they probably have a perspective of their own and are worrying about something completely different. If you are brave enough to wade in and tell your niece, sister or friend that her husband is a bastard and you would support her if she left him, you might be very surprised by her reaction.

Until the person concerned actually asks for your help, your difficult task is to hold your tongue and be prepared to pick up the pieces. This applies to those people whose friends are ruining their life through alcohol or drugs just as much as through their unsatisfactory relationships. The closer you are, the harder it can be. For many people their parents are the last people they would confide in. We don't want to burden our parents with our own grown-up problems until we have to. The GP cannot discuss the problems of a patient with someone else. If I found out that relatives had been to discuss my perceived marital problems with a solicitor (who wouldn't do it for free and, in any case, could do nothing), I would probably be furious. So beware. Unsolicited advice often results in heads being bitten off all round.

It is very important and not selfish to look after yourself when you are in danger of being drawn into the crises of others. Remember the instructions on the plane: First put the oxygen mask on your own face before you attempt to help others. This isn't the same as fixing things, but nothing is ever solved if the people looking on are dragged into the maelstrom along with the victim.

The best you can do for people you love who are in a difficult situation is to let them know that you are there if they need you. If you want to research the options open to them, then do so. Read books about divorce, ask people who have gone through it. Look into the work of Al Anon or the Citizens Advice Bureau. When the problem involves drugs or alcohol there are organizations that can help and give you advice, but you can't force somebody through their doors. Be prepared to offer friends a home, if necessary, but tread carefully. There is a fine line between interfering and simply letting someone know that you are on their side. There is also a danger, as organizations like Alcoholics Anonymous or Narcotics Anonymous could tell you, of disabling the person you love by denying them the chance to come to their own solutions.

Interfering in another's relationship is particularly difficult.

Relationships between two people are an intricate complex of needs and desires. At the heart of all relationships is a complicity, a something that keeps the people in it hanging on until one or other of the partners finds the situation unbearable and pulls away. A marriage between two people is a mystery not to be fathomed by those who only observe from outside. The cruelties we observe may be counterbalanced by moments of intimacy which we don't see.

So, to all concerned friends and families I say, hold back, observe and listen. Especially don't put your own life on hold while you wait for others to sort themselves out. Be prepared to offer shelter, lend money or give what practical support you can in a crisis. Let your loved one know, through whichever friends they might confide in, that you love them and will always be on their side. If children are involved, make sure they know they have a loving family round them. There is an exception. I would say that if you saw an adult's problem having ill-effects on children, then you would have a case for interference – but otherwise, our unenviable role is to watch and wait until we are wanted.

See also Fatal Loyalty, The Power of the People

Seven-step Dialogue between Parents and Adult Children

When I answer a reader's problem I always ask people to write in and say what they think, because I want to hear from people who might have been in the same situation and have something valuable to offer that I haven't thought of. When Rebecca wrote to me she told me she was the only child of a highly controlling and smothering mother who was a Holocaust survivor who had fled from Nazi Germany. These survivors and their children have very particular problems and there was a big response to Rebecca's situation, partly from organizations who specialize in helping these families but also from other adult children who have had to renegotiate their relationship with their parents as time has gone by.

The person I was most pleased to hear from was Alison, and the reason I was so delighted to get her email was because I had dealt with the problem she and her sister had had with their elderly, dependent father some months earlier. Their mother had died and their father – who wasn't close to either sister – had sold up his house and landed himself on the pair of them. Not unlike, as I pointed out, King Lear, and with much the same results. The sisters were not happy. I had some suggestions for helping their father to begin making a new life for himself, but the work was up to them. And here was Alison, writing in to tell me exactly what they had done.

At the heart of any renegotiation is the critical conversation between parent and child that aims to reset the boundaries. How on earth do you go about it?

Alison's father was not a refugee but he had made himself wholly dependent on her by parking himself in her home, and her problem was acute.

This is her experience and her seven-point guide, and she wanted to share it with Rebecca. Crucially, she worked on the basis that, however inadequate her father's way of showing it, he loved her deeply and would have been mortified to know that he was making his child unhappy. I print it here because all of us, at one time or another, have to face difficult renegotiations with the ones we love.

'First step,' wrote Alison, 'and the most difficult. Accept that you matter. Nothing can be achieved to find a balance before you believe that your wellbeing matters as much as anyone else's. Martyrdom is not attractive nor productive as a way of life. Resentment makes a vile life companion.

'Step two: I worked out very carefully, over a number of weeks, what was the minimum outcome I would be happy to accept. It was worth taking time because the answer evolved from something quite radical to something gentle and practical.

'Step three: I discussed this with my husband, close family and close friends. Partly to ease my conscience, partly to bolster my courage.

'Step four: I rehearsed over and over in my mind what I wanted to say and how I was going to put it. I prepared for questions and responses. I took all possible steps to avoid getting angry and emotional. In the two weeks leading up to this conversation I felt physically sick. It is important to acknowledge the physical difficulty and strength of these feelings and prepare.

'Step five: I took my dad to a nice quiet café. Instead of telling him he was "wrong", I explained from the perspective that I needed him to help me to help him. I told him kindly but honestly that I couldn't cope much longer with the way things were. He was surprised, simply because he hadn't seen matters through my eyes. But because he loves me, he was sympathetic. We agreed my family needed more space and privacy, and we agreed he might be happier if he made more effort to do things for himself.

'Step six: We agreed on timing for his visits.

'Step seven: (CRUCIAL) I accepted that, for a while, because he doesn't have the habit of doing things for himself, I will have to point him towards sources of information and activity. I'm enrolling him in a couple of social groups and have found travel companies that specialize in solo travellers.

'Please tell Rebecca that this took all my courage but I can't begin to explain how much lighter is my soul since I began. My father seems happier and I feel quietly proud of myself. All this can and should be done from love, not from anger, fear or guilt.'

I sent huge congratulations to Alison. And I wished very good luck to Rebecca. And I wish courage to anyone who is struggling with the basic human dilemma of shifting dependence between parent and child. If you are a parent, remember to take responsibility for your own happiness. If you are a child, however grown up, remember that inside your parent, however controlling, is another child. And don't begin to redress the balance without seeking help and support from others. The organizations I have mentioned at the back of the book can direct you to professional help if you need it.

See also Love and Peace, The Freedom of Forgiveness, Fatal Loyalty

Love and Peace

There is a growing practice, among those few people on the planet who have a great deal of money to lose, of entering into a prenuptial agreement. The many billions of us who do no such thing know about these agreements because we see them in the movies and read about them in the gossip columns. Prenups, as they are popularly known, seem controlling, pessimistic and untrusting to those of us who aren't film stars, but maybe it is sensible to divide up the spoils while the couple are full of warm feelings for each other. Dividing up the spoils in a spirit of resentment and bitterness only leads to more resentment and bitterness, huge legal fees and fewer spoils to divide.

The rest of us, who think we have no spoils worth dividing, are wrong. There are more things at stake than money. The accumulated emotional capital of a happy relationship is beyond valuation. It consists of happiness, contentment, support, security, productivity and deep peace of mind. It includes the greatest gifts of love, the gift of belonging and the gift of meaning. The loss of these when a relationship breaks up can be more painful than death itself.

Maybe there should be another kind of prenup. Not one that assumes defeat and divides the spoils ahead of time, but one in which both parties agree to face and resolve difficulties together in an agreed process which some call the Path to Peace. How I wish that I and my former loves had learned to listen to and negotiate with each other in this way. The precious emotional capital of a relationship is not usually lost in one cataclysmic coup, but squandered incrementally. An unhappy relationship rots from within over time, eaten away by the termites of anger, unkindness and mistrust. Signatories to a prenup of peace would have the means to shore up the relationship before it collapsed.

I first came across the Path to Peace in a workshop run by Seana McGee and Maurice Taylor. It is discussed in depth in their book, *The New Couple*. I was struck by the simplicity of the process in practice – because it is relatively quick to do. In skilled hands it takes minutes. And I was struck by its subtlety, because it acknowledges and provides a means of expression for the layers of other feelings that lie beneath the surface anger. By disclosing the bad feelings honestly, and getting them truly heard by the other, it also allows the hurt person to see their own part in the dispute. And it ends with both sides feeling understood, open and ready to communicate again.

In its simplest form, the partner who has a grievance to air suggests the Path to Peace and the other agrees.

In Step One, the speaker explains what has made him angry, and the other repeats his words back to him. For example, the speaker has been left waiting on the street because the other was late.

In Step Two, the speaker expresses the hurt and sadness that lie under the anger, and the other repeats his words back to him. For example, the speaker is upset that he was kept waiting because this made him feel unimportant and uncared for.

In Step Three, the speaker expresses the fear that underlies the anger and the hurt, and the listener repeats his words back to him. For example, the speaker is afraid that the lateness is a sign that his partner has lost interest in him and might leave.

In Step Four, the speaker acknowledges some responsibility for the problem and admits something he could have done differently. For example, the speaker admits he put pressure on his partner to meet him early, even though he knew she had a busy day.

In Step Five, the speaker expresses some understanding of what led the other one to behave as she did. For example, the speaker could acknowledge the fact that his partner has been working long hours lately and feels under pressure.

This may do the trick, but often there is more under the surface and the process may need to be repeated. Or it may stir something in the other partner and she may like to do her own Path to Peace. I watched a couple practise this – they moved from the woman's anger that her partner left the cap off the toothpaste tube, through her feelings about his disregard of her requests, and her fear that his sloppy ways meant he didn't care about her. Within minutes, they reached a reconciliation in which he obviously understood her underlying fears for the first time and they both felt heard and seen by the other.

There is another peace process I came across in *Teachings on Love*, a book by the Vietnamese Zen Buddhist monk, Thich Nhat Hanh. It is longer than the Path to Peace, but it provides a wise and skilful formula within which to express and resolve anger. You can also find it in his book, *Touching Peace*. Thich Nhat Hanh calls it the Peace Treaty, and it is practised at Plum Village, his retreat centre in France. It is too long to quote here, but it begins:

> *'In order that we may live long and happily together, in order that we may continually develop and deepen our understanding, we the undersigned vow to observe and practise the following.'*

I like this phrasing because it sets out what is at stake. We would all like to live long and happily with the ones we love most. The most successful couples have arrived at ways of expressing and resolving their differences and, if you haven't worked this out already, these two processes may help.

You may read about these techniques and think, 'I'm not going to go to all that trouble and make all that fuss. We can sort ourselves out.' You may be right. You and your partner may be naturally sunny and naturally skilled at handling the challenges of anger and disappointment and jealousy. I am not. Most of us aren't, and I know from experience that people who thrash about in the midst of fear and anger are like people struggling in a deep swamp. They get further in themselves, and they are in danger of drawing down anyone who tries to help them.

These peace processes are drawn up by wise people on the high dry ground of compassion and calm. They use these techniques in their own lives when they need to. The processes can be a lifeline to us people in the swamps if we use them well. They are particularly good for people who hate going on about emotions, because they are swift and effective and save days of recrimination and missed communication.

I think to be truly effective these practices need to be introduced in a relationship as early as possible, because no lifeline will save you from an emotional swamp that has deepened over years. Agreeing to use a peace process means that partners are committed to a double awareness of their own behaviour and their partner's feelings. This is living and loving consciously and responsibly, and it is the essence of mature love.

See also The Freedom of Forgiveness, Writing a Letter to God, Fatal Loyalty

Where Did I Go Wrong?

Ah, now you're asking. And if it is you that's asking, out of the depths of some crisis or despair, congratulate yourself. This is the turning point, the breakthrough, the moment where you start to learn, adjust and change. If the question you are asking is, 'Why me?' in a blaming kind of way, change your question unless you are prepared for some serious self-examination. Bad stuff happens to everybody. It's the people who want to understand *how* they contributed to their own loss or downfall who stand to gain something invaluable and who have the greatest chance of moving on.

You can go wrong in work, in friendships, in money, in love, in family relationships, and you inevitably will, sooner or later. What you want, short of restoring the status quo, which you probably can't, is to work your way to the point where you can say, 'That job loss / bankruptcy / illness / break-up was one of the best things that ever happened to me.' You won't feel like this in the midst of crisis, but the points where we go wrong are also the points where a whole new way of thinking and living opens up. I hope the following chapters help you get there.

Seven-step Broken Heart Recovery Programme

There is no agony like the agony of a broken heart. Nor is there any instant cure, though alcohol, drugs, geographical distance, workaholism and meaningless sex may numb it for a while. New love is the best palliative for a heart mangled by an old love, but rebound love is often a way of deferring necessary pain. A broken heart is another form of loss and grief. Loss and grief, unbearable as they are, always take time to heal. When you are lost in this awful, seemingly endless desert it may help to have a map of the unreadable territory you are in. When Caroline, Tony and other readers wrote to me out of the shock and pain of their broken hearts, it led me to map out a road to recovery. Nobody wants to have to tread this road, but millions have trod it before and millions will tread it after you. However bleak it seems, you are not alone. This is the Seven-step Broken Heart Recovery Programme and this is how it goes.

Step One: the Blow

Tony's lover says she no longer loves him. Caroline's lover admits he is still with his former girlfriend, and has been all along. Tracy realizes she no longer loves her husband and leaves him. Anna's lover, for whom she has thrown caution and a marriage to the winds, trotted out the old trite excuses: 'It's not you, it's me. I'm not worthy of you.'

Whatever. It's over. First you feel shock and numbness. Then the feeling floods in.

Step Two: the Devastation

Neil's wife left him after 25 years of 'what I thought had been a very happy marriage. Our separation came as a total shock. My total misery when she left cannot be exaggerated. For a while I was lost in misery and in fact I was very close to committing suicide and I would certainly have done it were it not for the support of my children and the fact that my wife would have inherited everything.'

Tony can't stop crying. His heart, and his sense of trust, are destroyed.

Amanda, who had already left her husband for the *coup de foudre* of her lover, went a bit mad and started incessantly phoning and stalking him.

'Initially I went on Prozac, started counselling, cried a lot on my own and to friends and went back to my long-suffering husband, who loved and forgave me.'

The Devastation is hell and the abandonment is made worse by the sense of betrayal and the loss of a glorious future. Once you have stopped crying you come to ...

Step Three: the Reaction

It is normal, as Trudy testifies, 'to go through a period of absolute grief and mourning for what had been.' Where you have been badly betrayed, the grief is twisted by rage, denial, the longing for revenge, the demonization of the lost beloved. Amanda, bad girl, who was her lover's boss, reacted by firing him. Lawyers are used as battering rams. Letters and clothes get burned. This is the triumph of unreason. Don't linger here any longer than you need to and avoid it if you can. Reaction is invariably bad.

Proactivity is so much better, but before you can go from reaction to proactivity, you need to pass through ...

Step Four: the Inward Search for Meaning

After the first round of rage and tears, the questions. Why you? Why him? Why her? What went wrong? What is wrong with you? Hours, weeks, possibly months and, if you are not very self-disciplined, even years of agonized self-analysis await you. Self-awareness is a good thing and proof that you have learned from bitter experience. Books can help. Amanda recommends 'a wonderful book by Doris Lessing called *Love, Again*.' I recommend, of course, my own book, *Everything I've Ever Learned about Love.*

Wallowing in prolonged and agonized self-analysis is a bad thing and will drive you and your friends mad. They may not like to tell you, so I will.

Put a limit on it. Move on, with calm deliberation to …

Step Five: the Forward Look

Take yourself in hand as though you were your own best and wisest friend. You could cram your diary with distracting activities. Things that take you out of yourself can be good. However, I like Trudy's more grounded approach, too: 'I'm really glad I didn't meet someone straight after my divorce because I would not have had the experiences I have had. There was a huge empty crevasse in my life but I didn't consciously fill it. I just set about savouring every moment, hoping to make the very best of life.'

Linda, having learned that 'I tended to pin my happiness on whether there was a man in my life validating me,' gradually realized that 'having a full social life, learning new things and opening your mind to other untried and untested experiences is very life-enhancing. Making mistakes is fine as long as you don't go on repeating the same ones – that's just madness.'

Once you have got a sense of the world beyond your own broken heart you are ready for …

Step Six: the Outward Search for Meaning

If you get this right it's almost worth having your heart broken. Behind you is one person, before you is the world and a fresh start. 'The truth is,' says Amanda, 'if you have been truly wounded it will never go away completely but you move on, make new relationships in a different circle.'

'I have a full life now,' agrees Trudy, 'with a busy social circle which I have made for myself. At potentially emotional times like Valentine's Day, I go out and buy myself a huge bouquet of lilies, and last Christmas I worked as a volunteer in a homeless hostel, which was one of the most humbling and rewarding experiences of my life. Wonderful things can happen if we have the stillness and quietness to see them.'

People who have learned to renew and reframe themselves are ready for …

Step Seven: the Whole-hearted Self

'Do I have a happy ending?' asks Linda. 'Well, naturally. Through my initial scattergun approach to socializing I developed a close circle of good friends who introduced me to a man who really loves and values me. Reader, I married him.'

Neil advertised in the personal columns and received 28 replies. He answered all of them and went to dinner with several. 'When I met Belinda we sold our houses and were married a year later. Since then my life has been wonderful. We have both had experiences we find it difficult to talk about, but communication is absolutely vital to the success of any relationship and my wife and I are entirely open about how we feel. Please tell people that there is life after separation and divorce, even later in life. I have never been so happy.'

And even without romance, there is happiness. 'We all have so much love to give,' writes Linda, 'and until and unless we find the one person, there are so many ways in which to give our love. We simply have to find what works for us and go out and do it.'

I couldn't agree more.

See also Set Your Compass to Love, How Do You Know When It's Over?, Fatal Loyalty, The Beauty Way, Singles and Their Habitat

How Do You Know When It's Over?

It's over when one of you says it is. It's as cruel and as clear as that. Love may be a consensus, but the end of love is often unilateral. I was reminded of that by the man I was helping to prop up the bar. He was going through a very bitter divorce. His wife had returned to her own country, taking their child with her, and neither the medical nor the legal system would give him any help. Slowly, and very expensively, he was losing both wife and child. I tried to say wise and comforting things, but the fact that his wife had refused all offers of conciliation, marriage guidance and counselling stumped me. She had decided it was over and everything after that was just damage limitation.

The commitment that counts is not the one you make to each other, but the one that both of you make to the relationship. More and more people are choosing not to marry, but the formality of a wedding in the public presence of your friends, family and community makes it very clear that a marriage is something built to overarch the temporary and fleeting feelings of the people within it. It is a structure designed to be visible from within and without, and to shelter its inhabitants from storm and drought, fire and plague. When one partner is down the other holds firm, and the beauty of the public commitment is that the wider community is complicit in this treaty. It is there to be called on when the inevitable difficulties arise.

When a couple disintegrates, the shock reverberates. It is not just about them. Parents and siblings are shaken. Loyalties have to be decided. Friendships and social circles can be torn apart. Children, if there are children, have their lives changed for ever.

Some couples stay together through enormous, heart-wrenching difficulties. They support each other through sickness and disablement, through poverty and debt, even through cruelty and abuse. If their commitment is to the relationship, they can even survive the trying periods of boredom and dislike. The glue at the centre is stronger than the pull to leave. It can hold together the most unlikely people but, when the end comes, it is often unilateral. It took two people to decide to be together. It only takes one to decide to go, and the couple is through.

The effect on the one left behind can be devastating, but the challenge is to accept reality. If you are the one left behind, whatever you are offering, it is not enough to counterbalance the pull of life outside the relationship. Whatever is in the balance against you – a new partner, a different kind of life, pure freedom – it has won.

It is only natural for this gravity to pull you, too. A time of break-up is a time of yearning and loss. It is also a time of anger and revenge. The yearning and the anger are both facets of your attachment to your lost love. They will both hold you in the past if you let them.

Survival at the end of a relationship demands that you identify and express the powerful feelings sweeping through you, but express them in a way that won't cause you or others further damage. Seek therapy if you are struggling on your own. Confide in friends. Above all, try to break the cycle. Beware of rebound relationships or you could find yourself repeating a pattern. Your ultimate goal should be restored self-worth and a new life so satisfying that you no longer care what happens to your lost love. I once met a very successful actress who had enjoyed sweeping past her ex's house in a new Rolls Royce. 'Success is the best revenge,' she purred.

This is a time to seek out old friends, to remember your best self. Lost love frees up lots of time. Don't just obliterate it with work or drink or drugs. Take some time to find out what else makes you happy, and explore it. You have time to excavate those parts of yourself that have maybe lain unused in this particular relationship.

Don't expect to go from shock and misery to happiness overnight. Depending on how deep your relationship went, it could take a year or two. But you can create islands of happiness in your sea of despair. And those islands can become stepping stones on to dry land. Dry land is where we look back at the sea of despair and our lost loves like so many boats on the horizon and wonder what we saw in them. Then one day, another boat may come along and, even if we're not ready for an ocean voyage, we can set off for a trip around the lighthouse. We're getting ready to sail again.

See also The Seven-step Broken Heart Recovery Programme, The Art of Self-reinvention, The Freedom of Forgiveness, The Power of Gratitude

Love vs Space – the New Infidelity

The end of love in the 21st century is space. Somehow it's supposed to be less insulting to 'need your space' than it is to criticize your lover. 'It's not that I find you boring, it's just that I need my space.' 'It's not that I don't fancy you since you put on ten kilos, it's just that I need some space.' 'It's not that our marriage is over or that I don't want children, it's just that I need some personal space to sort myself out.' And once sorted out, how many lovers, wives and husbands return to the narrow confines of the old relationship? Precious few.

Space is the new empire, the new nunnery, the new great excuse. It's where people retreat from love when they don't want to hurt someone, but they end up hurting them anyway – especially if their abandoned partner suspects that 'space' is just another name for the fitness instructor or that new girl at the office. Which it shouldn't be, by the way. Everyone recognizes space as the neutral retreating ground. So space is the perfect way to avoid the explosive confrontation that would happen if it really were the fitness instructor.

This is what happens if the need for space gets too desperate. It starts off small and ends up huge. It begins with a night on the sofa and ends on another continent. Space goes from a weekend away alone to a job in another town. Space grows from the garden shed to divorce.

If the one you love suggests they need more space, especially if it's a unilateral move, you may not have a crisis on your hands, but it's a warning to pay attention.

In an attempt to neutralize its power, space comes built into relationships these days. How many marriages now begin with Kahlil Gibran's words on love, from *The Prophet*?:

Love one another but make not a bond of love:
Let it rather be a moving sea between the shores of your souls ...
Sing and dance together and be joyous, but let each one of you
    be alone.
Even as the strings of the lute are alone though they quiver
    with the same music.

These words seem to offer a more manageable pattern for a contemporary relationship than the words of the Christian marriage service, with its challenging talk of 'for better for worse; for richer for poorer', and its promises to forsake all others. There is nothing there among those solemn words about negotiating space.

Space does have a lot to be said for it. The judicious use of space keeps many relationships going. Space is where you can sleep without being driven mad by snoring. Space is where it is permissible for one partner to go on a painting holiday while the other partner goes fishing. Space is what everyone needs to breathe and recharge. Space, in the right proportion, is what renews energy, appreciation and affection for the other. Space is good because people can choke to death from too much intimacy.

So how can you tell good space – the stuff that allows you to breathe – from bad space, the kind that will simply take your breath away?

Good space is negotiated. Bad space is stolen.

Good space ends up with two people being pleased to see each other. Bad space just turns into more and more space until your spacious lover disappears over the horizon completely.

So when the one you love says they want more space, it isn't necessarily the beginning of the end. But it could be, as Winston Churchill said, the end of the beginning.

See also Writing a Letter to God, The Freedom of Forgiveness, The Art of Self-reinvention, Making a Life with Meaning

The Enemies of Love

The enemy of love is not the temptation from outside. The enemy is always within. A successful couple has its own immune system. The world is full of diseases, but not everyone falls victim to them. The world is full of temptations, but not everyone is beguiled by them.

Bad habits and unhealthy self-destructive living can undermine our immune systems and make us vulnerable to attack from disease. In the same way, there are bad habits in relationships that create the conditions for turmoil and break-up. Happy people don't leave good relationships, but unhappy, dissatisfied ones do.

So the enemies of love are not the attractive work colleague or the sexy fitness trainer, the drinking companions or the mother-in-law. These are just viruses looking, consciously or unconsciously, for something to infect. The enemies of love are the forces within us that make us behave in unloving, neglectful or destructive ways. Neglect and indifference, by the way, are just as powerfully destructive and unloving as abuse and infidelity.

The enemies of love are contempt and the many ways of showing it, habit and the many ways of falling into it, inattentiveness and all the opportunities for intimacy and empathy that it misses. They are bad moods and the corrosive effect these have on other people, jealousy and its insatiable hunger for proofs, anger and its hydra-headed forms, from rage to cold silence.

The enemies of love are constant criticism and its infinite self-justification, nagging and its stupid inability to change tack, constant absence and the growing gulf it creates. They are lying and its destruction of trust, indifference and its irresistible power of erosion. They are unkindness and its deadly ability to wound and never heal, meanness and its stifling of all generosity. I am sure you can think of more.

All of these agents are the real forces of emotional destruction. Where they are uncontrolled, they are the death of love. They work away inside a relationship until all an outsider has to do is to knock at the door for the fortress to be breached. And in case you are thinking, 'Yes, I've known people who've behaved like that,' think again. I mean you. I mean me.

A sense of self-righteousness can be as big an enemy of love as all the rest. I have often been the agent and perpetrator of my own destruction. And so have you.

See also Love and Peace, The Freedom of Forgiveness, The Power of Gratitude

The Swamp of Complaint

I am ashamed to admit that there have been many times in my life when I have slid into the swamp of complaint and wallowed there, croaking. The swamp of complaint is the habitat that awaits you if you are incapable of making a change. You can detect its presence by the perpetual sound of moaning. You are old enough to enter it just as soon as you are old enough to grumble, so it could be as young as five or six, but most people become familiar with the swamp when they become teenagers.

What a perfectly wonderful and hospitable climate for moaning adolescence is. Once you discover that somebody else has impossible parents, nightmare teachers and unreasonable amounts of homework then you can start wallowing in your little mudhole of a swamp together. And the more of you there are, the bigger and more comfortable the swamp is.

You could climb out of it, of course, by doing something. You could get together to make sense of the homework and you could work out a way to negotiate with your parents or your teachers, but to do that you would have to give up something nice. You would have to give up the camaraderie and the sheer comfort of your friendly, companionable swamp.

I remember a swamp of complaint I joined in one of my early jobs. We had a difficult and capricious boss whose demands kept changing and could therefore never be met. At coffee breaks and lunchtimes we huddled together and moaned. We gathered in the canteen each day and bitched obsessively about what a nightmare she was. How cosy, how friendly and bonding those lunch breaks were, as we huddled over our well-worn complaints like labourers round a campfire.

I'm not sure that it ever occurred to us young rookies to do the grown-up thing, to climb out of our swamp, think hard about what the needs of the situation were and take a responsible part in meeting or even pre-empting them. Nor did we have the experience or the skills to confront our boss calmly and in a positive spirit in order to work out a way in which she could get what she wanted – fresh ideas and diligent research – without leaving us totally frazzled. So we stuck together and complained and in due course we left, I suspect just ahead of her decision to fire us.

When change comes to a group, be it friends, family, work colleagues or even a larger political grouping, there will be people, the majority, who dive, with a splash, into the swamp of complaint and stay there, making a lot of noise. There will be those who hang back, assess the situation and adjust creatively to the new reality. There will be a smaller group of people who are really far-sighted, see a much bigger picture and decide to make changes in their turn. And there will always be the happy, far-sighted rats who already have their exit strategy for leaving the sinking ship. The swamp is really the least creative and the least energized place to be.

As I have grown older I have become much more aware of swamps of complaint and how damaging they can be to the people in them. We jump in because we are in search of sympathy, but they suck us down. Now I recognize the signs. They are: becoming conspiratorial, endlessly voicing old feelings and points, never coming to any positive conclusion, talking behind people's backs but never to their faces, and voicing negative views without offering positive solutions.

I also know the best way to behave when you are faced with change you don't like. Take time to assess the new situation. If necessary, test your understanding by spelling it out to others to get their feedback. Work out what immediate and positive steps you can take to improve things. Come up with a list of ideas and seek a meeting, though only if you know the outcome you want from it and what you are going to do if you don't get it. Work out for yourself what your bottom line is if things don't go the way you would like. Are you prepared to leave?

Above all – and this is the difficult bit – resist the temptation to moan and grumble if you don't get an immediate solution. Either keep your counsel or seek out the company and advice of wiser and more experienced people. Ask for help with real situations, not just an indulgent ear for your fears and furies.

The swamp of complaint is a most seductive place, but no revolution was ever organized there. No great breakthrough has ever come from its depths. People who stay in swamps are overlooked and not respected. If you want to make changes, you have to climb out.

See also Making a Life with Meaning, Thinking Straight and Feeling Good, Knowing What You Want and Asking for It, The Power of Gratitude

Saving Yourself from Drowning

Farmers learn which clouds bring rain. Sailors learn to read the roll of a wave and a shift in the wind. Primitive peoples knew that their life depended on an acute listening to and observing of the behaviour of the skies around them. Weather forecasting was more than something that got you on television at peak viewing time. It was allied with shamanism and predictive power. The rainmaker was as important to a tribe as the deer-tracker or the storyteller.

We don't have to learn the arts of weather forecasting now because it's all there on satellites and computers, brought to us through television and the Internet. How many of us can recognize the shape of a rain cloud or know, instinctively, whether the wind is in the east or the west? We've lost our attunement with nature because we rely on umbrellas and central heating, but external weather isn't all there is. There's another kind of weather we can learn to read, and I think it is just as essential to our survival, on a personal level, as any ability to recognize the phases of the moon or the approach of a northwesterly.

I'm talking about inner weather, those moods and storms and hot spells that sweep through us and profoundly influence the way we think, feel and behave. We may think we are acting out of purest rationalism, but when we can see that the only logical way out of our dilemmas is flight or suicide, then our inability to weather-forecast our inner turbulence has led us fatally wrong.

People in the grip of anxiety and depression experience life quite differently from people who are in balance with themselves and life. If they lack awareness, they can't recognize that their unhappiness is the result of a transient chemical state. I mean this literally. I remember my father, a highly intelligent man who was prey to great anxieties, clutching himself miserably towards the end of his life and saying, 'We've had awful weather recently. Atrocious,' and shivering. The weather had been fine for days, but inside my poor father it was dark and stormy and cold. Because of his intelligence he could rationalize his own depressions as being the true state of things.

My father was my teacher in many, many ways. He taught me to love poetry and Shakespeare. He taught me to love the countryside and the layered history of the city. He taught me to have ambition and to think. But he also taught me how to make life miserable for myself. He was so articulate and so convincing that when he looked at life and always saw the worst, I believed, absolutely, that his view was right. It took me years to learn that there were people in the world who saw only the best, who didn't automatically look at any situation and immediately wonder what could go wrong. I thought that being pessimistic was the intelligent way to be.

It took me years to see that my father's fearfulness and pessimism were something peculiar to him and not a logical point of view. And it took me even more years to detach myself from them and create a world viewpoint for myself which is more hopeful. I have had to work very hard at states of mind which seem to come naturally to some people – like my mother, in fact, who is optimistic, pragmatic, not introspective and always cheerful and interested. She was born that way. I have had years of reading, therapy, workshops, seeking and searching for tranquillity, balance and peace of mind.

I have fallen a few times along the way. I once slid into a depression so deep that only medication could dig me out, but I was in therapy at the time and I still think it was the two weeks in Ireland that I took, in which I slept and read and walked endlessly on a wonderful beach, that restored me to balance with myself.

Since that time I have become a weather forecaster of my own inner state and I recognize the early signs of trouble. One is waking early in the morning, instantly awake and ravaged by dark thoughts. 'In the real dark night of the soul,' wrote Scott Fitzgerald, 'it is always three o'clock in the morning.' Or it might be 5 a.m., when, according to the poet Fleur Adcock, 'the worse things … stand icily about the bed looking worse and worse and worse.'

I won't have that any more. I switch on the light and banish them. I have so many things to do to control my inner weather that I put them all in a book, *Everything I've Ever Done that Worked*. My father read it. He said, 'Interesting but not for people like me.' The funny thing is, I said to my mother, the book's subtitle could be, 'How not to be like my father.'

I find the right Bush Remedies work: Emergency Remedy or, for obsessive worrying, Crowea. I recommend the Emergency Freedom Technique, which takes minutes to do – look it up on the Internet. For the long term I recommend meditation as the best training in recognizing your depressive thoughts and detaching from them. And, as a mantra, the Buddhist practice of seeing one's feelings as weather. At midday or 4 a.m., recognize your emotion as a fleeting state. 'Feelings of fear are passing through me,' you say and, as you repeat it, they will pass.

.

See also Thinking Straight and Feeling Good, Living Your Own Life, Making a Life with Meaning, The Power of Gratitude

Made in Error

I will never forget my first art lesson. I can see myself, at five years old, seated in front of a huge piece of paper with a brush in my hand and some unbearably exciting glass jars full of thick coloured paint on the desk before me. A teacher stood at the front of the class and she told us that we were going to make patterns. Patterns! I couldn't wait to begin. I plunged my brush into the glass jar of paint and made a lovely big square on the paper.

I don't remember what the teacher did next exactly, but I remember the paralysing shame. I had done something wrong. I had started before everyone else. I had started before she had explained what we were meant to do. I had made a big stand-out mistake and it was staring up at me from the middle of my spoiled paper. If a five-year-old can get any smaller, that is what I got.

If only somebody – preferably the teacher – had told me that it was OK to make mistakes. If only she had told me, when I was young enough to incorporate it into my life and play with the idea, that mistakes and unexpected changes happen to everyone. If only she had told me that life was simply crammed full of trial and error, mistakes and spoilings, choppings and changings, and the only thing that really mattered was how quickly and how creatively you could recover from them. If only she'd told me that the path of invention and science and art was littered with mistakes that turned out to be revelations and that human progress depended on them. But she didn't tell me anything like that. She just told me I was wrong.

I can remember exactly what my picture looked like to this day and how it was different from everyone else's. We were supposed to do repeating patterns, so I doggedly got on with making a repeating pattern and there was my inappropriate coloured square in the middle of rows of unadventurous and apologetic loops. As my mum said afterwards, it looked like a large crowd of people carrying a single flag.

Incidents like these can cut our creativity off at the roots and leave us afraid of making mistakes for the rest of our lives. Nobody tells us that Winston Churchill once defined leadership as 'going from failure to failure without losing enthusiasm'. Nobody tells us that the playwright Samuel Beckett urged people to 'Fail again. Fail better.' If they had, then we would have had an education in the art of taking things in our stride, and encouragement in escaping the deadening idea of perfection. The fact is, once you understand how creativity really works, you understand that there is no such thing as a mistake. Mistakes are better seen as errors, wanderings from the path, and truly creative people deal with these wanderings by incorporating them, using them as departure points and fresh stimuli to new possibilities. That teacher could have rescued me from shame and turned me round by showing me how I could incorporate my bold square into the patterns she wanted us to explore.

In the arts, error is encouraged. Actors go to improvisation class not only in order to loosen up their own creativity but also because things go wrong in live performance and you have to be free and spontaneous enough to keep going. It's no use Juliet freezing to the spot when Romeo forgets to feed her the right line. You might even have to improvise on Shakespeare.

Visual artists go wrong on purpose. I wish I'd known that when I was five. I wish I'd known that the Surrealists, in particular, devised all kinds of methods to bring the unexpected and unpredictable into their work. They wanted to lose control, not keep it.

I once went on a course run by Tate Modern on the art of mistakes and we were challenged to go away and create systems that would bring randomness and error into our own work. They could be anything from picking random words out of the dictionary to incorporate into a poem to cutting up a painting and rearranging it as collage. I heard of a woman who accidentally walked into a plate-glass window and used her accident as a basis for art, and another woman who turned her cancer X-rays into paintings.

Of course sometimes an error is a catastrophic change. It's hard to see how a surgeon can make a creative turnaround when he's taken out the wrong kidney, but using your cancer X-rays as a basis for paintings is a very powerful example of triumphing over disaster. As the writer Paul Virilio said, when he curated an exhibition devoted to accidents, 'Daily life is becoming a kaleidoscope of incidents and accidents, catastrophes and cataclysms in which we are endlessly running up against the unexpected.'

You can be sure that accidents will happen. That isn't important. What really matters is how we use them to keep going.

When unexpected change happens, a lifetime's experience of teachers and parents prompts you to say, 'Oh no!' But catch yourself out. Try saying, 'That's interesting,' instead. Or better still, 'What a fantastic piece of luck.'

See also Getting Conscious at 30, Writing a Letter to God, The Power of Gratitude, How to Be Creative

Now What Shall I Do?

So things didn't go to plan. You've tripped or fallen or you think you've failed. I don't think anyone is ever a failure, only a work in progress, so here are some strategies for moving forward. I hope you are inspired by the story of the old lady who walked to the mountain top to shed her despair after divorce. People often write to me wondering if it is too late to effect a change in their lives and, short of disability and death, I always say that it is not too late, ever, to make some kind of change that will restore your sense of wonder and possibility. It is hard work, of course. Perhaps I should have said that at the beginning. The most misleading words ever written were, 'and they all lived happily ever after'.

Somebody called Elbert Hubbard was nearer the truth when he wrote, 'Life is just one damned thing after another.' But he also said, 'There is no failure except in no longer trying.' In my job I hear from people in their seventies, eighties, even nineties, and they have the same problems as the rest of us – love affairs, family relationships, loss of meaning. And they are still carrying on searching for answers, still carrying on living, and I find that inspiring. Obviously we have to pace ourselves. Infinite adaptability is a life skill we all need till the day we die, and in the meantime we need to lighten up.

One great life skill is knowing the difference between banging your head on a brick wall or doing what I sometimes like to do, which is masterly inactivity. If life is driving you mad, stop. Put your problem to one side, write your letter to God, take a walk in the park and talk to a tree. It is amazing how a creative retreat can find the answer coming out of nowhere. My favourite tool is The Beauty Way (see page 149). You can do it anywhere. In the countryside, in the middle of a city street. It's a short cut to grace, which is why one of the final offerings in this book is just that, a touch of grace. It's to remind us that our life can turn on points of laughter and beauty and play.

Is It Ever Too Late to Change?

Dear Lesley,

I long to change my life but have I left it too late?

A despairing reader.

Dear Despairing Reader,

I have received this letter, in different forms, from readers in their twenties, their thirties, forties, fifties and sixties. It doesn't matter how old you are, you are never too young or too old to feel stuck or, hooray, to become unstuck. I have seen teenagers sobbing that their life is a failure and I have seen 90-year-olds begin an exciting new life in a whole different country. To the 90-year-olds I say, well done and thank you for being an inspiration. To the teenagers I repeat the 2,500-year-old words of the Athenian, Solon the Lawgiver, 'Call no man happy till he is dead.'

not a permission to commit suicide. That's a wry comment on the fact that life is an endless unreeling of twists and turns, successes and reverses, that continues to the last breath. We can't really make sense of it till it's over and, even then, it is left for those who are left behind to discern a pattern. This is not a matter for despair or joy, it's just how it is. So take a few deep breaths and remember the mantra murmured by a slave in the ear of triumphant Roman generals, 'This also will pass.' The good things pass and the bad things too. The important thing is to keep dancing.

Change is a subject I happen to have given a lot of thought to and, indeed, have written a book about, called *Everything I've Ever Learned about Change*. I wrote the book because I wanted to look at the way change works in a human life and how you can keep your head above water in the turbulence and even turn it to your advantage.

The first thing I want to say is that it is never too late to change, and I'm going to reinforce that with the experience of a reader who has written to me with her own solutions. Mary found herself divorced at 76 when her 81-year-old husband went off with a neighbour. I think that would flatten most of us into a state of perpetual semi-consciousness beneath the duvet. After all, at that age a lot of people would assume they'd had their last chance. It did flatten her, of course, but not for ever.

'I felt as if I was being consumed by all the negative emotions I was going through. I woke one morning with a decision filling my mind. I got up and cut about 25 small rectangles out of a piece of tissue paper. On each of these I wrote all the awful feelings – hurt, pain, betrayal, deceit, etc. – and put them in a plastic bag. Out came my climbing boots and I headed out to climb the fells. The sun was shining, the sky a clear blue and a frisky wind was blowing. When I reached a good height I stopped and, one by one, I held each piece of paper out in my hand and let it fly. I watched as each one lifted, fluttered, rose and flew. They blew out of my system and away.

'As I did this I thought, "This is just stupid," but since then I have changed. I feel released and relieved.

'I followed this by blowing some of my very scanty resources by going on an Arctic cruise, and there the space, silence, sea and, strangely, the lack of colour, brought solace to my soul.

'I came back from that trip determined to rebuild my life and I have! I have been accepted as a film extra and I am travelling the country, meeting lots of new people and new challenges and thoroughly enjoying myself. New beginnings indeed!'

Mary's story is so uplifting that it's worth looking at what she did right, so that those of you still sunk under your own duvets can get some directions for the path out of your misery.

First of all, when something really bad happened to her she didn't pretend that everything was fine. Instead of walking round like a lethal zombie, taking her suppressed emotions out on everyone around her, she acknowledged that she was feeling terrible and had enough intelligence and detachment to analyse and name the feelings, thereby reducing some of their power over her.

Second, she wrote the feelings down. If I recommend one thing in my books, it is the power of writing things down. The act of writing down clarifies a situation, detaches you from it, reduces its hold over you and often shows you the beginnings of a way out.

Third, she had a pair of walking boots ready to put on. If everyone had a pair of walking boots, and used them, how much happier we would all be.

Poets, scientists, politicians, peacemakers, soldiers and artists have walked their way out of trouble and into new solutions over millennia. As I mentioned earlier, there is a formula for problem-solving known as the three Bs – bed, bus and bath. These are supposed to be the places where people traditionally loosen their minds enough for new connections to be formed and new thoughts to float in. I added a fourth, beach, and now I would add a fifth – boots. When in doubt, get out of the house and walk; I promise you that your thinking will change and lift.

Fourth, Mary performed a ritual. As I once heard somebody say, 'If you want to make a change, make a ritual.' She created a symbol of what was troubling her – her pile of paper emotions – and she handed them over to something huge and elemental, the wind. The wind took them and absolved and released her. Some of you who write to me suggest your particular religious beliefs as the answer to all problems, but you don't have to subscribe to a particular religion to experience the power of harnessing something bigger than yourself – nature, art – as a partner in your life. The state of despair and stuckness is a solitary and isolated state. Ritual can take you out of it by reconnecting you with the flow of the world.

Fifth, Mary took a huge risk and expanded her horizons dramatically. She removed herself from her familiar surroundings and discovered a whole new world in the Arctic. She and I want you to know that this can be enormously liberating. In my book I describe the intoxicating effect that even a day away in unfamiliar places can have on your idea of yourself and your world. I recommend a day trip to Paris as a way of recasting your idea of yourself. She chose Greenland. Somewhere there is a place that will work for you, but even more important than the place is the act of going.

Sixth, she took another risk and knocked on the door of a whole new world of work. She doesn't say so, but in applying to be a film extra she was brave enough to take the risk of rejection, which is extremely scary. But bravery was rewarded. She wasn't rejected. She stepped into a new and exciting life at an age when too many people assume it's all over.

Seventh, please note that she changed her life in small steps, one at a time. This always works.

See also Stepping Stones, Writing a Letter to God, The Art of Self-reinvention, The Power of the People, Making a Life with Meaning, A Short Guide to the Subconscious

The Beauty Way

I first came across the Beauty Way of the Navajo in a book called *Finding Your Own North Star* by Martha Beck. It has been a constant resource for me ever since. I found that it has the power to transform my experience of the everyday, to shine the light of magic onto the most mundane, even ugly, surroundings. All that makes the Beauty Way one of the most extraordinary and powerful tools in my toolbox.

Here's how it works. I am stuck in my car in heavy traffic on a very unlovely through-road in a semi-industrialized soulless corner of south London. My body is cramped and uncomfortable. My mind is resistant and very resentful. My heart is down. I try reciting the Beauty Way:

There is beauty above me.
High white clouds are racing across a deepening evening sky. Their form and motion and free flow remind me of the westerly winds that are carrying them over the city from the open spaces of the Atlantic Ocean, over the green hills of

the West Country. They are beginning to catch the apricot warmth of the sinking sun. They draw my mind eastward, to the English Channel, the darkening fields of Belgium and northern France, even further east to the Russian mountains, where our icy east winds come from in winter.

There is beauty before me.
The tail lights of the van in front glow a rich fiery red. There is an abstract pattern in the flaking paint and rust. The dying sun is reflected in the tall glass wall of an office block ahead. Suddenly it stops being an ugly concrete block and becomes a stack of magic mirrors. The stalled traffic curves ahead, a serpentine line of smouldering red lights, to the traffic lights. Red – a rich luminous ruby. Amber – a warm, glowing orange. Green – an intense turquoise like the inside of an ice cave. Why hadn't I noticed before how beautiful traffic lights are? Everyday beauty, casually ignored.

There is beauty to the left of me.
A quick glance (I am meant to be driving). The car in the next lane is a gleaming abstract of reflections, a dark gleam of high-gloss paintwork, a slick of mirror, a transparent bafflement of glass which requires two lengths of focus, one for the dazzling surface, one for the dark interior. Why have I never noticed what a complex, subtle, mysterious object a car is?

There is beauty to the right of me.
To the right there is the same play of light on colours and reflective surfaces as the traffic streams past. As evening falls, a few headlights begin to shine, starlike, in the gleaming flow of metal and glass.

There is beauty below me.
It's hard to look down in a car and I certainly can't do it while I'm driving, but the lights turn red again. My eyes are caught and fascinated by the folded fabric of my own clothes on my lap, the subtle textures, the little canyons of light and shade in the pleats and creases.

There is beauty behind me.
A curving chain of lights is framed in my rearview mirror. The shape of the mirror itself miniaturizes and formalizes the abstraction of lights and tones, geometric shapes and subtle curves.

There is beauty all round me.
Yes, there is. Thank you.

There is beauty inside me.
There is. My anger and frustration have been transformed by the exercise of looking. What was a source of rage and impatience has become a source of fascination, pleasure and revelation. Of course I would much rather not be in a

traffic jam and I don't want to arrive rushed and stressed at my destination, but my experience has been wholly altered. I feel I have been given a priceless gift: seeing the world as a constant source of magic. I am awake and grateful.

See also How to Meditate and Why, Making a Life with Meaning, Saving Yourself from Drowning, The Power of Gratitude

When the Sea is Rough, Mend Your Sails

Sometimes nothing seems to be working. You're between jobs. You're in a relationship desert. You're trying to get projects off the ground but nobody is returning your calls. You should be training for a marathon, but you've turned your ankle. You're longing to move home, but deals keep falling through. You've reached the stage where you would even give up and go with the flow if you could, but there is no flow.

Sometimes life is just like that. If, when you look clearly at the situation, you seem to be making the right moves and the world isn't responding, it may be time to take the desperation out of your voice and eyes and respond to the deeper rhythm of events. You may have entered a period of winter. Winter isn't terminal, it isn't death. It's simply time to hibernate, to turn your energy inward and do your growing underground.

Westernized culture doesn't support hibernation. People lead global 24-hour lives where nothing ever sleeps. TV, radio, news, transport, light, heat, Internet all keep going like a funfair. Nothing switches off any more and life is full-on, or seems to be, so when it goes quiet for us it seems like a violation of the natural order, but it isn't.

Outside the industrialized, computerized world, whether you go back in time or sideways into different cultures, people understand the slower rhythms of life much better than we do. 'To everything there is a season,' says the Bible. Gardeners know it. Fishermen know it. Sailors, farmers, nomads know it. If you look closely at your own life you can see it, too. The rhythm changes. Sometimes things flourish, events pile up. Sometimes life feels as though it's gone into slow motion, even stopped.

I've found that the way to survive the little winters of life is to keep working but to reduce your activity and greatly reduce your expectations. At times like these it never works to force anything. When the sea is rough, mend your sails. When the ground is frozen, live off your harvest. When you can't take the herds into the pasture, give them hay and stay by the fire and weave your rugs or mend your tents.

Assuming you're not a fisherman or a nomad, there are plenty of things you can do in times of hibernation. These are times for editing your possessions, harvesting your resources, evaluating your progress, learning new skills, cultivating friendships, catching up on reading or sleep, caring for your body, going within and reconnecting with your dreams. There may be lessons to be learned and now you have the time to learn them. Your maps may need to be redrawn and now you have the time to redraw them, knowing all the time that the season and the energy will shift.

As spring follows winter, times of inactivity are followed by times where your feet don't touch the ground. A season in the wilderness, which can happen to the most gifted, famous and celebrated people, can quickly become a call back to the marketplace. And when the call comes, you'll be prepared, because one thing you do in times of inactivity is keep faith with yourself, your abilities and your dreams. You keep preparing, so that when the change comes, as it always does, you are ready to respond. And the next time the signs of winter come round, you can recognize and greet them without fear.

See also Making a Life with Meaning, The Power of Gratitude, Writing a Letter to God, Seven-step Broken Heart Recovery Programme

Thinking Straight and Feeling Good

One day the editor I was working for told me to go and see a psychiatrist. It's one of the joys of journalism that when you wake up in the morning you have no idea what the day will bring, but this was more off-the-wall than usual. She didn't think I was mad, but she wanted me to pretend I was.

What had happened was that the Priory, the private hospital of choice for burnt-out rock stars and addicted celebrities, was opening a branch near the City of London, aiming to catch burnt-out bankers and addicted traders. 'Book yourself an appointment,' said my editor, 'and write about what it's like.'

It didn't take me more than two minutes to realize that any good psychiatrist was likely to rumble a faking journalist in very short order. If I was going to do this job at all I was going to have to find a way to be truthful. So I found myself sitting in front of a highly qualified psychiatrist telling him the truth, which was this: that I was a journalist, that the previous year

I had suffered a period of clinical depression which had been treated with tranquillizers, and that I had also seen a therapist. I was no longer seeing the therapist and I had stopped the pills after three months, but the early symptoms of that depression – the disturbed sleep, gloomy thoughts and a feeling of dread in the pit of my stomach – were beginning to return. I didn't want to take any more medication, so did he have anything else to suggest and, by the way, did he know anything about cognitive behavioural therapy, because I'd heard it was good?

It turned out that I had booked an appointment with one of the relatively few psychiatrists in Britain who was also a trained cognitive behavioural therapist. In his experience, he said, it was effective and suitable for everything except psychosis.

Cognitive behavioural therapy is very practical and, unlike any other form of psychotherapy, it puts the techniques for change directly into the hands of the patient. Its premise is that bad feelings come from illogical thinking and that once you can identify your faulty thinking, you can counteract it. This well-tried process of self-analysis and correction will make the bad feelings go away.

Controlled trials have shown cognitive behavioural therapy to be as effective as medication for depression, and more long-lasting. Unlike other forms of psychotherapy it is relatively quick to take effect. No years lying on the couch remembering how mean your parents were to you – cognitive behavioural therapy starts with how you feel and act right now, this minute.

The nice psychiatrist offered me a few sessions to get started, which I didn't take because he also gave me the name of a book for the general reader, *Feeling Good: The New Mood Therapy* by Dr David D. Burns, based on his years of research at the University of Pennsylvania. I found the book in my local bookshop the same day and started doing the exercises in it, and that was all I ever needed.

I know exactly how depressed I was because one of the tools in the book is a depression index of questions which helps you grade yourself from mild to severe. If you are severely depressed – which, according to the index, means contemplating suicide and having worked out the means to do it – then please seek medical help. I was never that depressed, though I continued to use the book over the next couple of months until I realized I wasn't turning to it any more. It stays on my shelf as a valuable resource, even though I've not needed to use it again, and I recommend it to other people because, unlike many forms of therapy which often depend a great deal on the intuition, personality and skill of the therapist, cognitive behavioural therapy is extremely practical, structured and logical, and it works. If you prefer a person to a book, a search on the Internet will find you your nearest cognitive behavioural therapist.

See also How to Meditate and Why, Making a Life with Meaning, Saving Yourself from Drowning, The Power of Gratitude, The Beauty Way

Fatal Loyalty

Love is the most urgent call to self-knowledge. It is in our relationships with other people that we learn our shortcomings or test our powers of giving and unselfishness. Sooner or later, in many people's lives, these lessons become so urgent and so painful that people turn beyond the relationship and beyond their own social circle for guidance. It doesn't matter how cool or how experienced a person is. Secretly or overtly, they are always curious to know how this thing works.

It begins, in childhood, with the agony aunts. I remember the magazines with their problem pages hidden under the desk in the school library, telling us about problems we hardly knew existed. Now there are special problem pages for teenagers read by pre-teens, which talk about 'lurve' and give information on contraception and blow jobs.

The more practice you get, the more urgent is the need to accumulate knowledge and understanding as your mistakes get bigger and graver. Millions of people, over decades, have gone to marriage guidance or relationship counselling. Many of them learn what I learned, in a brief session of marriage guidance, which is how little we really listen to each other and how painful it can be when we really do. But if you want to learn even more about the workings of love in a relationship, then you need to know about far more than just what happens between the two of you. You need to become *archaeological*.

I have done two processes in later adult life that I wish I had done sooner. Both taught me profound lessons about the root sources of our ability to love, and how we can reclaim and reshape them. Both deeply affected my view of my family and my intimate relationships.

The first process is called the Orders of Love. It was originally developed by a German priest-turned-psychotherapist called Bert Hellinger, and it is now taught internationally. Its underlying thesis – developed over many years and synthesizing what he learned through working with the Zulu peoples of South Africa, and with further work in Western psychotherapies – is that love flows naturally through families and down the generations unless something happens to block it. Where there is an emotional problem in an individual, its cause is often a trauma or blockage further back in the family, which has distorted the flow of love. An Orders of Love workshop is an extraordinary and, to me, deeply mysterious and moving process, which involves participants nominating others to act out the roles of their family members and then watching as the unconscious drama unfolds. These groups of family members are called *constellations*. By physically positioning these people instinctively in relation to one another some alchemy happens, in which participants involuntarily express the emotions felt by the original family members, even though they know nothing about them. With the skill of the facilitator, who moves people about and brings others in, the original family trauma is uncovered. And then the facilitator creates a ritual of acknowledgement and forgiveness, which liberates the original participant from their family role of unconscious duty and loyalty.

The noble aim of this work is to break the invisible but sometimes fatal loyalties that bind families together, even in unhappiness, and break the chain for future generations. I have twice spent the weekend doing an Orders of Love workshop and been profoundly moved by the process. Taking part in other people's constellations feels like a great privilege.

There are connections between the work done by Bert Hellinger and his followers and the work done in the Hoffman Quadrinity Process, which is also taught internationally. Bob Hoffman's genius was to synthesize a number of forms of psychotherapy into an intensive eight-day residential process, which goes deeply into the way in which participants have learned about love through their families, and enables them to release the bad and deeply acknowledge the good. Both Hellinger and Hoffman acknowledge the intense and invisible power of what Hoffman calls 'negative love', that unconscious and self-limiting loyalty towards our families which leads us to adopt family roles and to suppress and sacrifice ourselves on behalf of family values, even when these are destructive. Hoffman also saw the human personality as being fourfold – an emotional, intellectual, physical and spiritual self – and the work focuses on giving each of these aspects of the self a voice, and integrating these aspects through the course of the week.

The Hoffman Process is longer, more intensive, more explicit, more structured and better designed to integrate into your life than the Orders of Love. It leaves you feeling exhilarated but also grounded, with a bag full of techniques you can use once you leave the workshop environment. It also provides you with valuable backup from the Hoffman community, and a network of participants who can help reinforce what you have learned. The experience of Orders of Love is less integrated into normal life, though it works well with therapy and is also profound, especially when you take part in other people's constellations and have the extraordinarily mysterious feeling of embodying the emotions of strangers.

Each time I have done an Orders of Love workshop it has made me deeply question the separate nature of the individual human personality. On the contrary, it has shown me clearly that we aren't separate at all. We are simply cells in one infinite human body, past and present and, in the right circumstances, the experience of one is the experience of everyone.

The boundaries between us are infinitely fine. This may be the message of the mystics, but in these two processes you can experience it.

Why would you want to give up your time and money to do this kind of work? I know that many people I meet, especially those who are disinclined to examine their emotions at the best of times, would rather break a leg than do what they would call 'wallowing' in emotion with strangers.

Well, why wouldn't you? Love is the central mystery and the greatest challenge of our lives. I read the story of a man who had nearly lost his life rowing across the Atlantic. He asked himself why he was prepared to face death on the open ocean but found his personal life so difficult. 'I think what it is is this,' he wrote. 'When you are involved with other people, lovers and loved ones, it's not in your control.' Somehow he found the challenge of the Atlantic simpler than the challenge of other people.

I can understand this. When I get it wrong in love the results can be devastating, for me and for other people. What I've learned through the work of Bert Hellinger and Bob Hoffman is that we are other people, and that knowledge is transformative. I have cried and laughed through these two processes, felt intensely, thought deeply. They have brought me some understanding and compassion, helped me open doors and mend fences in my own life, and given me insight into the roots of my own and other people's behaviour.

Love isn't a theory, it's an experience and, above all, a practice. In carefully evolved processes like these two, conducted by trained and responsible people, you learn about love through direct experience, and it can change the way in which you lead your life. What I also like about these two processes is that the people who run them aren't evangelical or pressurizing in any way. They only want people who really want to be there, doing the work when they are ready to do it. I wish I had found them earlier in my life. The details of how to contact these two organizations are at the back of the book.

See also Love and Peace, The Freedom of Forgiveness, Living Your Own Life, The Power of Gratitude

The Art of Self-reinvention

They taught me mathematics at school, and Latin, literature, chemistry, geography and physics. But no school – not even Hogwarts, where transformation is a daily lesson – ever teaches the essential art of self-reinvention.

If only they'd taught me, as I wrestled with 'What I Want to Be When I Grow Up', that you don't have to be only one thing. Not only that, you don't have to settle in only one place. You don't have to have only one job. You don't have to speak only one language or have only one hair colour or play only one instrument. You can be a constantly changing narrative of your own invention. You can be a multi-faceted, multi-skilled, complex, rainbow-hued, mercurial shape-shifter if you want. And even if you don't want, life may require it of you.

Nothing sharpens the CV-writing mind as keenly as the necessity of moving on, which is the mother of all self-reinvention. The sack and the divorce, once you've got over the shock, can be recast from disaster to huge opportunity to create another self, one that you've always rather wanted to be.

It's good to self-reinvent when you are young, because life hasn't defined you too sharply. And it's good to self-reinvent when you are older, because you have so much more material to play with.

The key jargon words are 'transferable skills'. I long ago passed the point where I realized I had somehow cultivated a whole garden of select facts about myself which I could cut and present like a custom-made hand-tied bouquet to any potential taker. Who do I want this person to think I am today? Am I going to emphasize my managerial-editorial-creative-artistic-musical-committee-member self? Do I emphasize all the travelling I've done (even though a lot of it was on holiday)? Do I make as much as possible of that newspaper job (glossing over the fact that I only had it for six months)? Do I knit together the experience I've had in fashion and design to make it look like a sustained and grounded career? Do I represent the accumulated years of acquaintanceship in my address book as a valuable network of contacts?

I do believe that we all have more to offer than we think we do. As a wild exaggeration, ambitious men tend to overpolish and overplay their hand. Women tend to self-deprecate. Neither is necessary. Self-reinvention, like moving the furniture around, is a skill you practise all your life and, in case you've got the wrong impression, I don't mean telling lies. Lies will find you out. I once read the highly embroidered CV of a secretary I worked with and you would have thought that she single-handedly made editorial decisions and upheld staff morale, when all she did was answer the phones and dispense coffee and sympathy. Still, hats off to her for sheer chutzpah.

Self-reinvention is an act before it becomes a story you tell others. It might need the conscious effort of acquiring an extra-curricular skill that you think would come in handy, but often it is done unconsciously through sheer *joie de vivre*. I think about the woman who learned Farsi for the intrinsic fascination of it and found herself working for a human rights organization in Afghanistan. I think of my mother, who has been a lifelong and devoted member of the Women's Institute and was commissioned to write a book about it, so she became an author in her seventies. I think about the friend who was a keen amateur musician for years and, when she lost her corporate job, moved into music management. I think about the friend who combined a keen interest in gardening with her experience in journalism to edit a gardening magazine and who is now the curator of a historic garden. It wasn't the linear career she planned when she first started planting her roof garden, but it's a fascinating life.

So, reinvent yourself. Do what you love. Move in the direction that draws you. Do something because you really want to. You can't lose. Your passions can become useful to you in surprising ways.

And each time you have to reinvent yourself you will find that the life you have lived is every bit as important as the job you have been paid for. What lies behind successful self-reinvention is the act of giving value to everything you have done.

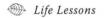
See also Writing a Letter to God, Making a Life with Meaning, Made in Error, Stepping Stones

In Praise of Self-help Books

Imagine you were faced with a huge pile of cardboard packing cases and that each time you ripped the sticky tape off the sides and tore one open, an old friend leaped out. The joy of reunion! The glad cry of recognition! That's what my life has been like for the last week as I have opened box after box after moving my books out of storage and into my new flat.

Books are friends. My favourite children's books are lifelong friends to be read in times of weariness and stress. I could never throw away *The Secret Garden* or *Through the Looking Glass*. Nor could I give away all my art books, or the books of poetry, the novels, the memoirs. And here are some very special friends, my collection of self-help books.

Saying that you have a collection of self-help books is like admitting to alcoholism or a serious chocolate habit: just not done in company. Which is why I am going to come right out of the closet and tell you that, yes, some of my best friends are self-help books. These books can offer you consolation and inspiration. They can articulate problems you had struggled to understand. They know how you feel and what to do about it. They give you strength, direction and, always, comfort. So I want to introduce you to some that have earned their place on my shelf.

I'm going to start with Tom Butler-Bowden. He had the brilliant idea of encapsulating the best in his guides, *50 Self-help Classics* and *50 Psychology Classics*. Just reading his summaries makes you feel better and tells you enough to decide which book would be best for you, right now.

50 Self-help Classics goes from the Buddha in the sixth century BC right up to the modern bestsellers like Louise Hay. Critics of self-help books attack them for being fluffily optimistic and glib, but Louise Hay's book *You Can Heal Your Life* has sold over 30 million copies round the world. That makes her the best friend of an awful lot of people.

As an advice columnist I sometimes recommend a self-help book to readers if I think it would help, and two I've recommended more than once are *Feeling Good: The New Mood Therapy* by David D. Burns and *The Happiness Hypothesis* by Jonathan Haidt. *Feeling Good* is the definitive succinct layman's guide to cognitive behavioural therapy, the down-to-earth therapeutic model that aims to sort out your emotions by getting you to examine your thinking. Its companion, *The Feeling Good Handbook* has added practical exercises.

The Happiness Hypothesis is a readable and inspiring synthesis of ancient philosophy on the art of happiness, backed up by current psychological and scientific research. Ancient philosophers and modern scientists agree that the way to be happy is not to acquire riches, status and possessions but to live a useful, virtuous and purposeful life. I much prefer this book to those self-help books which tell you you can have anything you want, especially riches, status and possessions, just by wanting them enough. No, my friends. Read Jonathan Haidt and understand that selflessness and contributing to the lives of others are much more likely to make you happy than the latest handbag. But you knew that, didn't you?

If loss of purpose and frustrated creativity are what bother you, I recommend Martha Beck's galvanizing book, *Finding Your Own North Star*, and Julia Cameron's hugely popular guide to nurturing your own creativity, *The Artist's Way*. Martha's voice is a friendly one, and Julia is inspiring. She'll have you over-riding those voices that tell you you'll never paint a picture or write a novel. I was very happy to unpack my copies of *The Artist's Way* and Julia's follow-up books, *The Vein of Gold*, *The Sound of Paper* and *Finding Water*.

And what about those books which are even quieter in their voice than these? Sometimes a book is a place, a sanctuary to open and enter when the outside world is too noisy and fast. These are the books which are more spiritual guides than self-help mentors. I discovered *Finding Sanctuary: Monastic Steps for Everyday Life* by Abbot Christopher Jamison quite recently. It is lucidly and lovingly written, and although it is based on Christian practice it is specifically designed for anybody who wants to create a quiet and contemplative area in their life. When I am in search of calm and perspective I also find I return to the books of the popular Buddhist writers, particularly Thich Nhat Hanh and Pema Chodron. Thich Nhat Hanh writes simply and beautifully about meditation, and the very titles of Pema Chodron's books show an understanding of the madness of people's daily lives. Two of the best known are *When Things Fall Apart* and *Start Where You Are*. Another good book on meditation is *Turning the Mind into an Ally* by Sakyong Mipham Rinpoche.

Finally, I was very happy to unpack my own books, particularly *Everything I've Ever Done that Worked*, which is still my personal guide to all the techniques and practices that dig me out of my own particular holes and re-inspires me. I forget, we all forget, what works, which is why we need to see it written down. With all these friends out of their boxes and up on my shelves, I feel I can face the world.

See also Making a Life with Meaning, My Samurai Partner, The Power of the People

The Freedom of Forgiveness

I would be a hypocrite if I said I found this easy. I just know that, along with the practice of conscious gratitude, forgiveness is the most important step you can take towards peace of mind and emotional freedom.

Life offers us innumerable opportunities to practise resentment, nurture hurt, replay grievance, simmer with justified anger, burn with betrayal. These strong emotions can consume us utterly. There have been times in my life when somebody has hurt me and in my constant replayings of the drama I have been the wronged one and they have been anywhere on the villainous scale from incomprehensible to downright cruel. If you think of yourself as a nice person, you simply long for others to repent of their evil ways and see things your way. If you aren't troubled by being nice, you may just want to kill them.

I've learned that the only way to survive with grace is to forgive. Nobody is hurt by your pain and anger but you, and the more you repeat the pain within yourself, the more damage is done. Take appropriate action by all means – this isn't about being a passive victim. Decide what results you would like. Make your feelings known, write a letter of complaint, even put the matter in the hands of the lawyers if you must, but emotionally let it go. There's no victory if you win your day in court and still feel bitter.

Of course you will find it hard, even impossible, to do this at first. The shock and hurt of being a victim can last a very long time, even a lifetime, and simply saying words of forgiveness will have no immediate emotional impact on you at all. If there is deep and lasting damage you may find relief and support in professional therapy. But if you begin the practice of forgiveness, it has the power of the drip of water that wears away the stone.

My friend Gloria Karpinski taught me an inner ritual of forgiveness. Imagine an altar of light. Imagine putting the person you need to forgive on this altar of light. Say, 'I forgive X for all sins against me, real or imaginary, in this life or any other.' Imagine the person dissolving in the light. Then place yourself on the altar and say, 'I forgive myself for all sins against X, whether real or imaginary, in this life or any other.' Or the words of the Lord's Prayer may be enough for you, if you reawaken their meaning: 'Forgive us our trespasses, as we forgive those that trespass against us.' Whatever our spiritual tradition, forgiveness is demanded of all of us.

We can practise forgiveness on a daily basis because we are injured on a daily basis, even in small ways. When somebody cuts you up in traffic, enrages you over the telephone or is rude in a shop, don't fume, don't seek to hurt back. Above all, don't escalate and reproduce the hurt. Imagine surrounding the person with light and mentally say, 'I forgive and release you.' Even imagine blowing them a kiss – lightening this up with humour is a very good idea. And move on.

Without forgiveness I can tell you what happens. It is not the unforgiven who suffers. It is the person who can't forgive who carries the wrong, the hurt, the injury unhealed and constantly reactivated. That person is the one whose mind and body are in danger of being permanently damaged by pain, bitterness and resentment. Life is too short to suffer and be held by the past in this way. The practice of forgiveness, even when the wrongdoer continues to do wrong, is the only way to freedom and peace.

See also The Power of Gratitude, Seven-step Broken Heart Recovery Programme, Made in Error, Living Your Own Life

The Research and Development Fund

Big companies have research and development funds. Individuals seldom do, but without a research and development fund it can be difficult to change your life.

I think the single most valuable thing that money can buy, apart from health, is the time in which to have a life-changing experience. I don't simply mean time learning new skills and acquiring knowledge, though this is a wonderful thing and I can never have too much of it. I mean time in which life itself can teach you.

There are changes which happen in a heartbeat, but considered change takes time. And it often takes money. Here is a dream situation. You have worked steadily for some time and you have built up a reserve fund which will allow you to take time out of your career to retrain, or to follow a passion, or to volunteer in a field that interests you, or to travel in pursuit of a dream. Of course you might have cleaned up on the stock exchange instead, won the lottery, backed a winning horse or inherited a large sum of money from a distant relative. These are all possible, but I really don't recommend counting on any of them. Creating your own fund is the way to go, but create it with a purpose. Know what it is for.

A research and development fund can buy you books that will help you change your life. It can pay for you to take an evening class or go on a weekend course, even take a part-time degree. It can allow you to travel and explore, not just to take a holiday but to travel with a purpose, to research archaeology, practise a foreign language or do voluntary work that will help someone else and re-educate and re-energize you. More and more employers are recognizing that staff who take time out to re-energize themselves re-invigorate the workplace, too. A research and development fund can pay for a whole year off when you wake up and realize that you've been doing the same job without a break for far too long.

When I was 50 my research and development fund rescued me from an intolerable feeling of being stuck and sent me off to art school. When I look back at my diaries I can see that those first few weeks of art school brought me alive again. I was thrilled with the stimulation, the tapping of latent creativity. I loved the sociability of working alongside other people whose minds and spirits and lives were in a state of flux. I loved being taught how to see again. My research and development fund bought me new friendships as well as time away from my habitual life, a new level of knowledge and expertise and, in due course, new paid work.

If you are poor to start with, or young, which often amounts to the same thing, there are other ways to create the leverage which brings change in a research-and-development kind of way. You can try stepping stones (see page 65). I know, for example, someone who was determined to get into radio. She had a job as a newspaper reporter which had begun to bore her and she'd done an evening class in radio which had inspired her. Against the advice of her family she threw up her job so that she would be free to do unpaid volunteer work in community radio and unpaid work at her local radio station. She earned her keep by spending nights working in a bar, and cut her expenses by taking a bed in a shared room in a shared house.

It all looked grim to begin with and she worked very hard, but over the course of a single year she began to get paid shifts in radio and progressed to the point where she was doing so many of them that she could give up the bar work. Then she moved from paid shifts to a short-term contract and finally became a member of staff, earning double what she had been getting in her newspaper job and becoming more skilled because of the invaluable technical training she was getting. There were plenty of risky points along the way, but this woman created her own fund of time and effort, and her commitment impressed her future employers so much that eventually she benefited from the organization's research and development fund and not her own.

Research and development may not even need a fund. It can happen in very small spaces if it must. Julia Cameron, in *The Artist's Way*, recommends artists' dates, weekly outings where you go alone into the world, take the pressure off yourself and stimulate your imagination. You could take a walk in the park, go to an art gallery or spend an hour on the beach.

I know an editor who makes all her staff stay at their desks through the lunch hour. Nobody likes working for her and their creativity and enthusiasm dry up. I know another editor who hates to see her staff at their desks in the lunch hour. She wants them out on the street seeing the latest art exhibition, picking up ideas from what people are wearing and checking out the shops. She's not daft. That is all research and development. And it not only keeps her and her staff in touch but also keeps her magazine on the ball.

Left alone, doing the same thing over and over, we stagnate and freeze. If life isn't changing for you, then it is vital to create the conditions for change yourself. Having a research and development fund of your own, whether it is £50 or £500, is the best way I know of being your own guardian angel.

See also The Beauty Way, When the Sea Is Rough, Mend Your Sails, Is It Ever Too Late to Change?

Set Your Compass to Love

What is your inner compass set to? Are you aware of having an inner compass at all, or are you helplessly buffeted by the wind and weather of emotion, the victim of external forces from the moment your feet touch the ground in the morning to the moment you embrace the dark of night?

Try setting your compass to the true north of love. When your eyes open at daylight, do you love what or who you see? Do you love the face on the pillow beside you? If you do, lucky you. If not, why are they in your bed at all?

If you are the only person in your bed, do you love your sheets? The colour of your walls? The objects on your bedside table? The pattern of your curtains or the view from your window? If the answer is no, you might feel a bit depressed. It might be difficult to change the person in your bed or the view from your window, but it is not at all difficult to change your curtains or your sheets. Once you start to make a conscious choice and choose things that you love, a profound change can be set in motion.

William Morris said we should not have anything in our homes that we do not find to be useful or believe to be beautiful. Here is my counsel of perfection: Do not have anything in your life that you do not love.

Make love the most over-used word in your vocabulary. Let it kick out routine and habit. When you get dressed in the morning, do you love your underwear, your shoes, your fragrance, your ties, your clothes? Did you buy them because you loved them or because you're stuck wearing a uniform, or because you thought they were cheap or inoffensive or useful and would cover your lumpy bits? Do you love the way they make you feel, or do they make you feel comfortably invisible?

Do you love what you eat for breakfast or is it a mindless habit? Do you have an activity you love to look forward to at the end of the day, or do you watch television? Do you really love watching television? Do you love your neighbourhood or is it just handy for transport?

You get the idea. Every single waking moment of our lives offers us choices we can exercise through love, and the simpler the choice the easier it is to make it with love. We can choose to build love from the ground up, instead of grasping it out of some future sky.

I love fresh flowers. I love the bunch of daffodils I bought for less than a pound, which sits in a blue jug I love, on the faded tablecloth I love because I bought it on holiday, spread on the wooden table I love because I fell for the grain and sheen of its surface. This cumulation of simple objects kick-starts my day each morning.

My act of love is the act of attention that takes each object in and acknowledges its place in my life. I can swallow a bowl of cereal inattentively or I can sit at my table and enjoy it slowly, appreciating the blue-rimmed china bowl I eat it from, enjoying the company of my jug of daffodils and the view of the clump of bamboo in my garden which I can see bending in the morning wind. I love the bamboo and the way it dances. I love the fact that I planted it from a pot and it is now a little grove of stems that give me shade in summer.

If there are people at my breakfast table I can grunt at them from behind the newspaper, which I admit I often do, or I can perform that act of attention, of gratitude, that consciously takes in their presence, listens to what they say, gives thanks for their company. If I have started my day with love I have a small head start on the brutal forces of indifference and chaos that wait for us all. And I have also tuned myself to recognize and experience love in the confusion and variousness of the day ahead. If my inner compass is set to love, I may get lost a thousand times, but it will always guide me home.

See also The Beauty Way, Relating to the World, The Power of Gratitude, Being Your Own Best Friend

A Touch of Grace

I kept changing my mind about how to end this book. I wanted to leave you with something inspiring and uplifting and practical, too, but nothing seemed quite right. So I took the manuscript on holiday to Ireland with me, knowing and trusting that I could get it right if I let it sit for a few days fermenting while I walked on the beach, breathed fresh air and slept a lot.

It wasn't until inspiration struck that I realized I was practising what this last piece preaches. Sometimes you work too hard and the work just becomes counterproductive. At that point, letting go and playing are the things that can make all the difference. This applies to life as well as to books.

On the last two days of my holiday I felt ready to look at the manuscript again but, even on the last day, I got stuck in the same place. So, on my last night, in a small seaside town in the southwest of Ireland, I went for a stroll by the sea after dinner. I felt calm, rested, ready to return, but there was still a piece of the jigsaw missing.

The weather in Ireland had been unsettled, with some very heavy rain, and as the sun set behind me, the foot of a rainbow grew from the hayfields across the bay. I stopped to admire it as it climbed into the cloudy sky and then vanished, and then I turned and walked towards the sea. Far out on the horizon my eye was caught by a misty pink spot on the rim where sea met sky.

I couldn't understand what it was and, as I watched, it slowly grew into another mysterious, vertical shaft of rainbow, surging like a fountain from the slate-grey surface of the deep. And as it climbed into the sky I saw, enthralled, that another parallel rainbow began to bloom by its side. And then they too faded.

So I turned, still marvelling at what I had seen, to walk back to my hotel, and that was when I was completely arrested by the transformation of sky and bay behind me. Yet another rainbow, huge and complete this time, arched right over the hills towards the sea, and at its feet the fields were dissolving into the thick gold light thrown by the setting sun. As I stood in amazement, a second rainbow bloomed and grew outside the first, until everything I looked at was sheltered by a perfect double bow.

When you see a natural phenomenon of such completeness and perfection it defies language, but as I stood there, stupefied with delight and gratitude, one single word came into my mind: 'Grace'.

Of course, I suddenly thought. Of course. Grazia; grace. That was what I was receiving and that was the end of this book, and that is what I wish for you. This piece, 'Decoro, Sprezzatura, Grazia' is from *Everything I've Ever Done that Worked*. It is a suggestion for how you can live your life with grace, and it was the crock of gold I suddenly found at the foot of all those Irish rainbows.

Decoro, Sprezzatura, Grazia

In 1991 I sat in a rehearsal room in Sapporo, Japan, with the dying Leonard Bernstein and had a conversation about the relationship between inspiration and hard work. Bernstein was nearing the end of his life and he was very sick, but I'd just watched him electrifying the London Symphony Orchestra through a rehearsal of Sibelius's First Symphony. Now, with a large Scotch in one hand and a forbidden fatal cigarette in the other, he lay exhausted in the corner of a sofa and talked about the way in which he identified with the composers whose music he conducted. If he'd done his preparation thoroughly, he said, he absorbed the score into his very bones. He could feel that he was composing Beethoven and Mahler anew in the performance. He became the music.

I had an idea to swap with Bernstein, one I'd been given by Anthony Rooley, lutenist and specialist in early music. I told Bernstein that he was talking about the art of *Sprezzatura*, and once I'd explained it to him, he agreed.

The musicians of the 17th century, Rooley told me, believed that a great performance had three elements: *Decoro*, *Sprezzatura* and *Grazia*.

Decoro is all the preparation and hard work. It's the lonely research, the checking, the rehearsal, repetition and often futile-seeming effort and drudgery which prepare the ground.

Then comes *Sprezzatura*. It is the art of spontaneity. It is the art of standing on the hot spot and performing with such invention and freshness that it is as though the work is flowing through you for the first glorious time. It is the experience of being inspired. This is exactly how Bernstein said he felt about the music he conducted.

Sprezzatura is impossible without *Decoro*. Imagine a mountain. *Decoro* – hard work – is probably nine-tenths of the climb. *Sprezzatura* is the peak – it's magnificent, but you don't hang about there for long. And *Grazia* – divine grace – is the blessed light which illuminates the summit. *Grazia* is what touches a performance in which *Decoro* and *Sprezzatura* are in perfect balance.

But this theory applies to far more than musical performance. It is a Theory of Everything. Leonard Bernstein's life, as I wrote when he died three months later, was a perfect illustration of how these three elements can be the essential ingredients of a successful life as well as a memorable concert. He had astonishing talent but he worked like a dog. His performances, even his rehearsals, were full of *Sprezzatura*, spontaneous to the point of shock. And many people, millions, can testify to the *Grazia*, the grace, that his work teaching, composing and performing brought to their lives.

You don't have to be a kind of genius to use these elements in your life and work. They apply to every kind of human endeavour, from sitting school exams to throwing a party to fighting a campaign. *Decoro* without *Sprezzatura* will not do. It is no more than uninspired plodding. But *Sprezzatura* without *Decoro* can lead to the leap which misses the trapeze, the blazing but unprepared talent destroyed by nerves, the dazzling lawyer tripped up by the unexpected question. No *Grazia* there.

Work and play are both essential to human endeavour, but I know from experience that the work comes first. Anyone who has become deeply involved in a project knows that moment when a brilliant creative solution suddenly appears after hours, days or even weeks of labour. Or as Sam Goldwyn said, 'The more I work, the luckier I get.' The luck is *Grazia*. You only get it when you know how to work and then play.

Resources

This book grew from original material based on my 'Lifeclass' column in the *Daily Telegraph*. Other pieces have been reprinted from my earlier books or taken from my column in *Easy Living*.

From *Everything I've Ever Done that Worked*: The Power of Gratitude, How to Meditate and Why, Writing a Letter to God, Knowing What You Want and Asking for It, The Magic of 20 Minutes, Make Friends with Money, The Beauty Way, When the Sea Is Rough, Mend Your Sails, Thinking Straight and Feeling Good, The Freedom of Forgiveness, Decoro, Sprezzatura, Grazia.

From *Everything I've Ever Learned about Love*: How to Stay Married for 60 Years, Singles and Their Habitat, Love and Peace, How Do You Know When It's Over?, Love vs Space, The Enemies of Love, Fatal Loyalty, Set Your Compass to Love.

From *Everything I've Ever Learned about Change*: A Short Guide to the Subconscious, Stepping Stones, My Samurai Partner, The Power of the People, The Swamp of Complaint, Made in Error, The Art of Self-reinvention, The Research and Development Fund.

Thank you to Susie Forbes, editor of *Easy Living*, for permission to use the following columns: Relating to the World, Saving Yourself from Drowning, In Praise of Self-help Books.

The two courses I recommend in Fatal Loyalty (page 161) are the Orders of Love and the Hoffman Quadrinity Process. For more information on Orders of Love or constellation work, look on the websites www.constellations.co.uk and www. ordersoflove.co.uk.

The Hoffman Institute at www.hoffmaninstitute.co.uk regularly runs residential processes in the UK and abroad. Tim Laurence's book *You Can Change Your Life* (Hodder & Stoughton) gives a clear account of the process developed by Bob Hoffman and the thinking behind it.

In emergencies I always recommend people to contact the following organizations:

For relationship difficulties, whether or not you are married or in a couple, www.relate.org.uk.

For despair and loneliness, at any time of day or night, www. samaritans.org.

For problems with alcohol, www.alcoholics-anonymous.org. uk.

For drug addiction, www.ukna.org.

For the worried relatives and friends of people with addictions, Al Anon at www.al-anonuk.org.uk.

Hay House Titles of Related Interest

Hay House Titles of Related Interest

You Can Heal Your Life, the movie,
starring Louise L. Hay & Friends
(available as a 1-DVD set and an expanded 2-DVD set)
Watch the trailer at www.LouiseHayMovie.com

*****

Everything I've Ever Done That Worked, by Lesley Garner

Everything I've Ever Learned About Change, by Lesley Garner

Everything I've Ever Learned About Love, by Lesley Garner

Froth on the Cappuccino, by Maeve Haran

You Can Heal Your Life, by Louise L. Hay

We hope you enjoyed this Hay House book.
If you would like to receive a free catalogue featuring additional
Hay House books and products, or if you would like information
about the Hay Foundation, please contact:

Hay House UK Ltd
292B Kensal Rd • London W10 5BE
Tel: (44) 20 8962 1230; Fax: (44) 20 8962 1239
www.hayhouse.co.uk

***

Published and distributed in the United States of America by:
Hay House, Inc. • PO Box 5100 • Carlsbad, CA 92018-5100
Tel.: (1) 760 431 7695 or (1) 800 654 5126;
Fax: (1) 760 431 6948 or (1) 800 650 5115
www.hayhouse.com

Published and distributed in Australia by:
Hay House Australia Ltd • 18/36 Ralph St • Alexandria NSW 2015
Tel.: (61) 2 9669 4299; Fax: (61) 2 9669 4144
www.hayhouse.com.au

Published and distributed in the Republic of South Africa by:
Hay House SA (Pty) Ltd • PO Box 990 • Witkoppen 2068
Tel./Fax: (27) 11 467 8904 • www.hayhouse.co.za

Published and distributed in India by:
Hay House Publishers India • Muskaan Complex • Plot No.3
B-2 • Vasant Kunj • New Delhi – 110 070.
Tel.: (91) 11 41761620; Fax: (91) 11 41761630.
www.hayhouse.co.in

Distributed in Canada by:
Raincoast • 9050 Shaughnessy St • Vancouver, BC V6P 6E5
Tel.: (1) 604 323 7100; Fax: (1) 604 323 2600

***

Sign up via the Hay House UK website to receive the Hay House
online newsletter and stay informed about what's going on with
your favourite authors. You'll receive bimonthly announcements
about discounts and offers, special events, product highlights,
free excerpts, giveaways, and more!
www.hayhouse.co.uk